THE MALAY DILEMMA

MAHATHIR BIN MOHAMAD

THE
MALAY
DILEMMA

Mahathir bin Mohamad

TIMES BOOKS INTERNATIONAL
Singapore • Kuala Lumpur

Cover photograph courtesy of Jabatan Penerangan Malaysia

Published by Times Books International
an imprint of Times Editions Pte Ltd
Times Centre
1 New Industrial Road
Singapore 1953

Times Subang
Lot 46, Subang Hi-Tech Industrial Park
Batu Tiga
40000 Shah Alam
Selangor Darul Ehsan, Malaysia

Reprinted 1970, 1973, 1977, 1979, 1981, 1982, 1983, 1985,
1989 (twice), 1992, 1993, 1994

Printed in Singapore by Magenta Colorprinters Pte Ltd

ISBN 981 204 355 1

Why We Publish This Book

This is an important book because it is written by an educated, progressive Malay, and because it deals frankly with the problem of racial harmony in Malaysia, where roughly half the population is Malay and half non-Malay. We are publishing it because we believe the author's views should be read — whether or not we share them.

Dr Mahathir sets out to give his interpretation of the Malays' point of view. He is fully entitled to do this, though not all Malays will agree with his explanations or his opinions. Dr Mahathir, for years, was an important member of the United Malays National Organization. He was expelled shortly after the 1969 General Elections (in which he lost his seat) because of his open criticism of the present Malay leadership.

This book seeks to explain the causes for the 13 May 1969 riots in Kuala Lumpur, to explain why the Malays are economically backward, to explain why the Malays feel they must insist upon immigrants becoming real Malaysians speaking, in due course, nothing but Malay, as immigrants to Australia speak English, as immigrants to America speak nothing but the language of what the author calls "the definitive people".

Dr Mahathir argues that the Malays are the rightful owners of Malaya, that immigrants are guests until properly absorbed. He makes the point that immigrants are not truly absorbed until they have abandoned the language and culture of their past.

Dr Mahathir is pessimistic about the future. He believes it is not entirely out of the question that "ultimately, political power might prove the complete downfall of the Malays". At the same time he considers that removal of all protection from the Malays (which at present they enjoy because of political power) would subject the Malays to the primitive laws that enable only the fittest to survive.

v

Dr Mahathir's solution is a sort of "constructive protection" worked out after careful study of the effects of heredity and environment. Until this is done, he says, the deleterious effect of heredity and environment on the Malays is likely to continue.

Dr Mahathir expects that some of his explanations and contentions will be utterly unacceptable to many Malays. He believes he has a right to express his sincere and honest opinions, and he does so in the belief that he is helping to contribute to a solution of the Malaysian problem.

This book is important because of that, and it is of interest beyond Malaysia and the Far East because it deals with the problem of human beings of different races living together in the same territory.

Contents

Contents

1: Introduction

My early thoughts on problems affecting the Malays were first set down in arguable form in response to a challenge made by Professor Ungku Aziz, Professor of Economics (now Vice-Chancellor) of the University of Malaya. In 1966, at a seminar in Kuala Lumpur discussing the reasons for the poor examination performance of Malay students, I brought up the question of hereditary and environmental influence as being among the factors contributing towards the problem. Admittedly a lot of other factors such as education policy, poor facilities, inadequate and inadequately trained teachers play a part in producing the high percentage of failures among Malay students. But, in my view, hereditary and environmental factors cannot be dismissed lightly.

This view was generally disapproved by the seminar participants and in particular by Professor Ungku Aziz, because it was thought to imply that Malays are by nature inferior, and that this inferiority is hereditary and consequently permanent. This is not what the writer implied or concluded. The intention was to spotlight certain intrinsic factors which retard the development of the Malays, particularly those which can be corrected. If it is known and admitted that there are certain practices which are harmful, then it would be easier to suppress them.

Generally speaking, modern ideas on the evolution of man are not acceptable to Muslims and therefore to Malays. But even Malays admit that certain characteristics are passed from parents to offspring. *"Bapak borek, anak berintek"* is a well-known Malay saying which means "A spotted father begets a speckled son". The meaning is obvious. If this is so for an individual then hereditary influence must play a role in the development of a collection of individuals which constitutes a race. What is not generally known by the Malays is the effect of in-breeding.

1

In this book I have explained how the laws of genetics, which govern the transmission of hereditary characteristics, are affected adversely by in-breeding and other marriage practices.

There has been a lot of scientific thinking on the subject of in-breeding and the effect on human society. Cyril Dean Darlington, a British geneticist, in his book, *The Evolution of Man and Society,* takes the extreme view that the evolution of human society is the product of genes. According to him, civilizations flourish and decay in obedience to genetic decrees. He pointed out that once a ruling class fixed itself in power, it sought to conserve that power by in-breeding, thus denying the infusion of fresh stock. It was this habit, according to Darlington, that expedited the decline of the Pharoahs, the Ptolemies and the Caesars.

This interesting hypothesis is perhaps too extreme to be generally accepted even by non-Muslims. In any case, Darlington was referring mainly to incest, a practice which is unknown among the Malays. However, the modern definition of in-breeding includes marriage between first cousins and other close relatives, a practice fairly common among the Malays. Hereditary influence also produces an adverse effect in a society which, abhorring celibacy, insists that everyone, fit or unfit, should marry. Thus, the deformed in mind and body are somehow paired off and reproduce.

While it must be admitted that in-breeding is not general among the Malays, what cannot be denied is that the instances of in-breeding are greater among them than among the other major race in Malaysia — the Chinese. In fact Chinese marriage custom specifically prevents in-breeding. And so it is correct to say that in-breeding together with forced marriages of the unfit produce a much greater percentage of human failures among Malays as compared with other races.

This explanation is offered in mitigation and defence of my views. Nevertheless it is not expected that they will be easily accepted. The implications are too depressing and hold no promise of easy or rapid remedies.

The environmental factors affecting the Malays are less controversial. It is easier to blame extrinsic rather than intrinsic factors. Besides, environment is more easily corrected and unlike hereditary influence, holds greater promise of easy adjustment.

Having discussed some of the factors that affect the evolution of the Malays, it is only logical to proceed to identify and analyze the other causes which contribute towards putting the Malays in the peculiar position in which they now find themselves. Rupert Emerson, writing of the Malay authorities of Kedah in his book *Malaysia,* remarked that "(they) are condemned to fight a series of rearguard actions from each of which they emerge shorn of some element of their former autonomy." What was true of Kedah Malays seems to be true of other Malays. Now, as before, the Malays seem to be teetering between the desire to assert their rights and arrogate to themselves what they consider to be theirs, and the overwhelming desire to be polite, courteous and thoughtful of the rights and demands of others. Deep within them there is a conviction that no matter what they decide or do, things will continue to slip from their control; that slowly but surely they are becoming the dispossessed in their own land. This is the Malay Dilemma.

The publication of this book is not calculated to endear the writer to any particular section of Malaysians. Indeed, it is most likely to cause despondency among some, and severe resentment among most others. No apologies are offered. What I have written is written with sincerity.

Mahathir b. Mohamad

Pondok Maharizan
Batu 6, Titi Gajah
Kota Setar
Kedah
1970

2: What Went Wrong?

What went wrong? This is the question that anyone sympathetic to or interested in Malaysia must be asking since 13 May 1969. What went wrong in a multiracial, multilingual and multireligious country which for twelve years had enjoyed racial harmony and cooperation, that tolerance and understanding could be so abruptly terminated and the various races should sullenly glare at each other and reject a way of life that apparently began long before Independence? What went wrong that the Malays and the Chinese, the major races of Malaysia, could be so divided that not even the presence of an authoritarian Government and the efforts of national leaders could heal the rift?

What went wrong? With the benefit of hindsight it is of course easy to point out the flaws and the mistakes of the past. Nevertheless it is useful to look back and analyze, and even apportion blame, if the past is to be a lesson for the future. It is not vindictiveness but an exercise in social responsibility to try to explain what went wrong. For certainly if everything in the past was right and everyone was blameless, there would have been no disruption in the even progress and comparative racial harmony that characterized the first twelve years of the independence of Malaysia.

In order to know the causes of the present inter-racial disharmony in Malaysia, it is necessary first of all to examine the "harmony" that existed before. Was this harmony real and deep-rooted? Did it have a solid basis? Was there any difference in the relationship between Malays and non-Malays during different periods in the history of Malaya? What was the true relationship between the races during the years immediately prior to 13 May 1969? Did other factors contribute to the outbreak of violence?

Looking back through the years, one of the startling facts which must be admitted is that there never was true racial harmony. There was a lack of inter-racial strife.

4

There was tolerance. There was accommodation. There was a certain amount of give and take. But there was no harmony. There was in fact cacophony, muted but still audible. And periodically the discordant notes rose and erupted into isolated or widespread racial fights.

Racial harmony in Malaya was therefore neither real nor deep-rooted. What was taken for harmony was absence of open inter-racial strife. And absence of strife is not necessarily due to lack of desire or reasons for strife. It is more frequently due to a lack of capacity to bring about open conflict.

The Malays and the Chinese may live as neighbours. They may meet each other in their daily business and even socially. But when they retire, they retire into their respective ethnic and cultural sanctum, neither of which has ever been truly breached by the other. And in their own world their values are not merely different, but are often conflicting.

If it is accepted that there never was true racial harmony, then it is easier to trace the relationship between the Malays and the non-Malays through history and explain why inter-racial strife occurred. It may even be possible to work out a system to overcome the defects due to the type of relationship which had existed and so enable, if not harmony, at least a diminution in the areas of conflict.

Prior to the coming of the Portuguese, there were non-Malays in significant numbers in Malacca and Kedah. Of these quite a number were Chinese. Relationships between Malays and Chinese were, as far as can be ascertained, cordial. This is easily understandable, because whenever the Chinese are in a minority, they always avoid provoking the Malays. (This also explains why racial fights in Malaysia never occur in states like Kelantan, Trengganu and Kedah.) It is almost certain that they endured certain indignities without complaining too much, even though China claimed suzerainty over the Malay states. The Chinese and other non-Malays acquired not only the language but also the way of life of the Malays. Conflicts were therefore rare and never sustained.

5

The coming of the Europeans greatly increased the influx of non-Malays, especially Chinese and Indians, into Malaya. The impermanent character of their stay in Malaya made them a people apart, never really coming in contact with the Malays. This lack of contact minimized conflict, although towards the later part of British rule the Malays became more and more conscious of the danger the Chinese and Indians posed to their political power in the country. Sporadic minor Sino-Malay quarrels occurred, but the firmness with which the British dealt with these prevented any serious outbreak of inter-racial strife. Besides, Malay rights to the country were never openly challenged either by the British or the immigrants in the Malay states.

Under British rule the Malays lived physically apart from the Chinese and Indians, coming into contact with them only for brief periods during the day. Large sections of the Malays in the countryside hardly met the Chinese at all, and the same could be said of the Chinese in the larger towns and the tin mines. There were no significant racial clashes, but it is wrong to infer that there was racial harmony or even tolerance. People who live apart need not like each other. If there was no conflict, it was because there was no occasion for confrontation. There was only a consciousness of each other's existence, and this consciousness was sufficiently unpleasant to prevent any desire for closer relations. The seeds for conflict were in fact already there, though prevented from germinating by the authority of the British.

The Japanese occupation served to separate the Malays from the Chinese even more. Certain sections of the Malays were actively pro-Japanese while the rest were, if not sympathetic, at least not anti-Japanese. The Chinese were naturally discriminated against by the Japanese, while the Indians identified themselves with the struggle to liberate India. Towards the end of the war these relationships were somewhat changed. A large number of Chinese collaborated and gained the favour of the Japanese, while the Malays, not being too useful to the Japanese, were ignored. Whatever their relationship with the Japanese, the distinction between the races was emphasized and they were mutually antagonistic.

Thus when the British returned, the Sino-Malay relationship was anything but cordial, and when the Communists (mostly Chinese) tried to set up a Government for each of the Malay states, bloody Sino-Malay clashes were precipitated. These clashes would have developed into a racial war, but for the arrival and imposition of the British Military Administration backed by the full weight of the British Armed Forces. The Communists were frustrated in their attempt to take over Malaya, while the Malays, unsuspectingly, welcomed what they thought was a return to the pre-war relationship with the paternal British.

They were soon disillusioned when the British proposed to give the Chinese and Indians equal rights with the Malays in a new Malayan Union. Once again Sino-Malay antagonism was heightened, but this time it was rationalized and sustained by the conscious support of the Malay masses. From that time on Sino-Malay attitudes became national politics, to be dealt with not at local levels but by the highest authority in the land.

Although the British proposal did not go through, its effect on the Malay-non-Malay relationship was prolonged. Not even the most respected Malay leaders could overcome Malay antagonism towards the non-Malays. Dato Onn (founder of the United Malays National Organization) was eased out of the United Malays National Organization because he proposed to cooperate with the non-Malays.

However UMNO under Tunku Abdul Rahman experimented with Sino-Malay cooperation in the Kuala Lumpur Municipality elections in 1952. The result was sufficiently encouraging to make the Malays forget some of their misgivings. The experiment was again tried on a larger scale in the 1955 general elections, and the success of this ushered in a honeymoon period during which inter-racial cooperation was genuine. True harmony was still wanting, for each race thought that the marriage was one of expedience. It was during this honeymoon that Independence was achieved.

This briefly is the historical background of race relations in Malaya prior to Independence. Only during the period immediately preceding Independence was there some semblance of harmony between the races in Malaya. Prior to that, what has often been carelessly referred to as racial harmony was in fact a negative quantity — the absence of open conflict. And this absence of conflict was due more to extrinsic rather than intrinsic forces.

Nevertheless the atmosphere of 1957 was full of hope. Sino-Malay cooperation in seeking independence seemed to have paid off well. The Government of newly independent Malaya undoubtedly had the backing of the great majority of Malayans of all races. The opposition was weak and divided, with only one representative in the highest legislative body. The racial partners within the governing Alliance were aware of the recent history of conflict and were careful to avoid thorny racial problems. Besides, they were committed to the promises and agreements which had been reached prior to the achievement of Independence specifically to minimize racial antagonism.

But power corrupts, and the near-absolute power that the Alliance obtained corrupted the thinking of the leaders almost absolutely. UMNO, the mainstay of the Alliance, held more power and therefore has to accept the major share of responsibility for the decay which gradually affected the Alliance government almost as soon as Independence was achieved. What finally led to the outbreak of violence on 13 May 1969, started the moment the Union Jack was lowered and the Malayan flag went up. In a burst of enthusiasm the people of Malaysia bestowed upon the architect of Malayan Independence, Tunku Abdul Rahman, the title of Bapa Merdeka. The title was apt and was no doubt sincerely given to honour the man most responsible for the achievement of Independence.

UMNO, like all political parties, has a constitution which provides for the proper regulating of its functions. There is a specific policy-making body whose work is carefully laid out beforehand. The Central Executive Council is the highest authority within the party, but, powerful though it is, it is expected to work with the sanction of the general body and not against it. It may decide contrary to the wishes of the general body at times. This it is allowed to do because of the extra and probably secret information which is available to it. But it cannot consistently ignore the opinions of the general body of members. In order to give the ordinary members a channel for voicing their opinions, supreme authority is vested in the General Assembly of Representatives which must meet at least once a year or whenever the need arises.

Unfortunately, when the leaders of the party also became the highest and most authoritative officers of the Government, the provisions of the party constitution appeared incompatible and even irrelevant. The prestige and authority of these officials as members of the Government outweighed those of party officials. The Prime Minister in particular became so powerful both by virtue of his office and by popular acclaim, that the party became subservient to his person. And so, not only was the General Assembly frequently put off, but even the Central Executive Council was not called upon to discuss Government policy or even party policy. The party was held together not because the members had generally identical ideas on politics, but through a system of patronage and disguised coercion based on Government rather than party authority.

Patronage and coercion can only have effect on people who are directly exposed to them. The majority of the ordinary party members were not so involved that they could be affected by these systems. As patronage became more and more indirect, as when a village was denied or given development projects, it became more and more difficult to elicit favourable responses. In other words, the return for the investment in patronage became less and less predictable as it became more and more indirect. Patronage is therefore self-limiting and no replacement for true popularity or intrinsic similarity of ideas and aims.

The advent of patronage as a factor in intra-party politics was significant, for it meant that the leaders were no longer answerable to the ordinary members and the faceless supporters, but were only answerable to themselves. A feeling of power normally grips those who wield patronage, a feeling that they can mould and shape people and opinion any way they please. The leaders of UMNO, the senior partners of the Alliance Government, succumbed to this disease and, believing that they no longer needed to heed the opinions of their supporters, they disregarded them at every turn.

When it came to power, UMNO had more strength than it needed. The repeated disregard for intra-party criticism did not seriously impair its strength at first. But nevertheless the continuous whittling away of its mass support steadily told on its ability to garner sufficient support during elections.

UMNO came into being because of the Malay fear of losing out to the Chinese. The honeymoon period immediately before and after Independence lessened this fear, but it was never really absent. For, so long as the Chinese, or at least the fairly numerous adherents of the Malaysian Chinese Association, cooperated, this fear remained subdued. But the gradual divergence of the leaders from the stated policies of UMNO, and the continuous and more forthright demands of the Chinese within and outside the MCA, soon awakened the old fears. UMNO leaders chose to appease the Chinese, depending partly on the power of patronage and the usual docility of the Malays to keep party followers in line. But the decision to disregard the mild criticisms, and the failure to appreciate the steady defection of supporters soon had its effect. UMNO weakened, until by the time of the 1969 elections, its strength had so eroded that it had to rely on promises of huge discriminatory Government spending in order to gain support in some stubborn areas.

One would have thought that the more intelligent members of the Government would have recognized the signs. The Sino-Malay quarrels in Bukit Mertajam in 1964, and the Hartal Riots in Penang in 1968, were plainly indicative of the trend. But the Government was apparently oblivious to what went on around it. Secure in its absolute majority in Parliament, it was openly contemptuous of criticism. Policies were made which completely ignored public opinion. Typical of this was the decision to use Government funds to settle the cost of a private summons case when a Minister sued an opposition MP for slander. The decision was made after the case was lost. If the Minister had won he would no doubt have collected the damage awards.

Another example was the answer in Parliament to a query as to why a Malaysian Consulate should be established in Taiwan. The Prime Minister said, among other things, that the relationship with Taiwan would facilitate the visit to that island of some Ministers who seemed to find Taiwan very congenial. Ministers are no doubt human, but to dismiss an important policy criticism with this frivolous remark, showed the utter contempt of the Government for accepted public morals and public expectation. Laws were hurriedly passed without prior consultation with the representatives who had to "sell" these laws to the people. Tax innovations were made and discarded with complete disregard for the disrupting effect on the public. In the main, Parliamentary sittings were regarded as a pleasant formality which afforded members opportunities to be heard and quoted, but which would have absolutely no effect on the course of the Government. The general feeling was that whether or not the Parliament sat, the Government would carry on. The sittings were a concession to a superfluous democratic practice. Its main value lay in the opportunity to flaunt Government strength. Off and on, this strength was used to change the constitution. The manner, the frequency and the trivial reasons for altering the constitution reduced this supreme law of the nation to a useless scrap of paper.

A newly independent country needs, above all, superior skill at the helm of Government. Decisions have to be made every day, and these decisions affect the country and the people. The Ministers and the Cabinet are vested with this decision-making authority. It is obvious that only the most capable and experienced should be made Ministers and be in the Cabinet. But independent Malaya chose to treat membership of the Cabinet as a reward for loyalty to party chiefs and acceptability to the Prime Minister. Once appointed, no amount of dereliction of duty could affect the position of a Minister. On the other hand, even if the Minister performed well, failure to remain on good terms with the Prime Minister meant removal from the Ministry.

The result was that mediocre men were left to run the country. The capable ones never got into the Government and even if they did, they did not stay long. As Cabinet after Cabinet was formed and the same pattern continued, the whole nation gave up hope that the Government would ever be made up of the truly able. The people became cynical and respect for the Ministers was minimal. This feeling did not merely pervade those who were opposed to the Government, but also those who supported the Government.

As can be expected, these Governments of mediocre people were bereft of ideas, were unable to understand the limits of their authority, and were generally unable to rule. A formula generally used to counter criticisms was to appoint commissions to study and report. The work of these commissions, usually composed of able public figures, normally took time. This gave the Government breathing space. When finally the reports were made, the Cabinet found difficulty in studying them. A new committee would be appointed to study each report. More time was consumed. When finally the Cabinet made a decision on the report, whole chapters were rejected and the implementation of what was left was put off indefinitely. In effect, the work of the commissions was a futile exercise and a waste of public money and time. The Government carried on very much as if no commission was appointed at all.

All the while however the Government was busy on devices to perpetuate itself. These devices were so transparent and so lacking in subtlety that they achieved just the opposite effect. Everyone except the Government saw this. Thus, long after the rural development schemes had lost their impact, the Government still carried on building mosques and community halls, not because these facilities were thought necessary, but in the mistaken belief that it would favourably influence the voting at the next election. As was to be expected, as an election approached, the grants for these rural development schemes increased. Until just before and during election, the Ministers were kept busy handing out cheques. The recipients of this largesse made a great show of gratitude, but it was apparent to those who cared to observe that their sympathy was not automatically with the Government. But the most damaging thing about these hand-outs was the discrimination in favour of known party supporters or party strongholds. This blatant partiality evoked the most bitter resentment against the Government and ensured that those opposed to the Government remained permanently so. On the other hand, as the Government could not possibly meet all the requests of party supporters, there was an ever increasing disillusionment with the party and more defections.

It is clear that by the time the 1969 elections approached, all sections of the people were disenchanted with the Government. The Malays were disenchanted because in their eyes the Government continually favoured the Chinese and had failed to correct the real imbalance in the wealth and progress of the races. In airing their grievances they antagonized the non-Malays, especially the Chinese. The Chinese demands increased as Government concessions whetted their appetite. At first, Chinese moderates thought that the demands of the chauvinists were useful to keep the Malays in check, but soon the moderates became the victims of their own strategy. To retain their influence they had to fall in line with the chauvinists. Needless to say this antagonized and revived the distrust of more and more Malays. The cleavage between Malays and non-Malays was thus being continually and inexorably deepened.

Over and above these racial reactions was the increasingly diminishing faith in the ability or desire of the Alliance government to rule and rule well. Although it was generally accepted that only the Alliance could be in a position to rule the country, the need to give it absolute power was questioned. The opposition parties were poor alternatives and did not really win adherents, but the general

13

disgust with the Alliance brought about a degree of anti-Alliance feeling. This was sufficient to produce an avalanche of protest votes.

Then the final blunder was committed, a blunder to cap all the faults and lackadaisical attitudes of the past. Believing that the strength of the Alliance Party lay in its wealth and its subsequent ability to conduct a prolonged campaign using not only party officials and ministers but also a huge army of paid workers, the Government opted for a protracted campaign period. This permitted the racial grievances which had been building up over the years of Alliance rule to come to the boil. Against the violently communal appeal of the opposition parties the Alliance had no answer. Worse, the Government found itself unable to stem the worsening racialist trend in the campaign. The only people the Government was able to control were members of the Alliance themselves. Thus when an UMNO publicity officer in Penang was battered to death, the Government was completely successful in preventing a demonstration. But, when a Labour Party member was shot the Government failed completely to stop a major show of defiance.

The Election results were a shock to the Alliance Party and the Alliance government. Uncertain of its authority in Selangor where it managed to win only half the seats, the Government permitted a victory procession of the opposition parties. Considering the show of defiance during the Labour party funeral only a few days before, it is difficult to see how the Government could have expected anything but trouble if the opposition was allowed to hold a victory procession. The Government had always been cautious about public demonstrations of any kind in the past. The elation of the opposition over the election results was obvious, and past experience had shown that leaders of the opposition had never been really able to contain the exuberance of their followers. In allowing the procession the Government demonstrated a failure to judge the mood that gripped the opposition as well as the supporters of the Government. The Government must therefore accept a share in the blame for what followed.

What went wrong? Obviously a lot went wrong. In the first place the Government started off on the wrong premise. It believed that there had been racial harmony in the past and that the Sino-Malay cooperation to achieve Independence was an example of racial harmony. It believed that the Chinese were only interested in business and acquisition of wealth, and that the Malays wished only to become Government servants. These ridiculous assumptions led to policies that undermined whatever superficial understanding there was between Malays and non-Malays. On top of this the Government, glorying in its massive strength, became contemptuous of criticisms directed at it either by the opposition or its own supporters. The gulf between the Government and the people widened so that the Government was no longer able to feel the pulse of the people or interpret it correctly. It was therefore unable to appreciate the radical change in the thinking of the people from the time of Independence and as the 1969 elections approached. And finally when it won by such a reduced majority the Government went into a state of shock which marred its judgement. And so murder and arson and anarchy exploded on 13 May 1969. That was what went wrong.

3: The Influence of Heredity and Environment on the Malay Race

How do hereditary factors affect the development of the Malay race in the Malay Peninsula? No truly scientific study has ever been carried out. It is perhaps kinder to leave this subject alone as it might prove rather discouraging to the Malays. But as hereditary factors are so important in race development, it is far better to shed some light on them so that a better understanding may lead to overcoming, at least partially, the adverse effect of these factors.

This does not pretend to be a scientific study. At best it is an intelligent guess. It is hoped that it will generate a new interest in this subject and perhaps lead to a comprehensive scientific evaluation of the theories propounded. At the very least it will serve to focus attention on an important subject.

That hereditary factors play an important part in the development of a race is an accepted fact. It does not need a scientist to point this out. Quite obviously if family characteristics are passed from father to son, racial characteristics must also be passed from generation to generation. If this were not so, then a completely different race would emerge every generation. But as racial characteristics throughout each generation are as distinguishable as family characteristics, it follows that these characteristics are hereditary.

Long before science took an interest in inherent traits, men had already noticed and accepted that offspring must carry some of the distinguishing characteristics of their forebears. Most obvious of course are features. Children are expected to, and do, resemble either one or the other of the parents, or even both. But resemblance to the parents does not stop at physical features. Character, intelligence and even inclinations tend to follow those of the parents.

Nevertheless, these similarities are not exact. Some characteristics are exaggerated while others are mere traces. Again, there is often a blending or a cancelling out of certain characteristics of both parents.

As the ordinary man's observation is limited in time and depth, it is left to the scientists to delve further into the mysteries of heredity. The most celebrated of these scientists, Gregor Johann Mendel, systematically studied the existence of hereditary factors and their transmission through genes. His findings have become widely accepted. Briefly, Mendel's Law states that offspring are not intermediate in type between the two parents, but that the type of one or the other is predominant according to a fixed law. The importance of this law lies in its rejection of the popular concept that offspring must be a dilution of the opposing characters of the parents.

Mendel's Law is best illustrated by experiments in breeding white and brown mice. Provided that a sufficiently large series of experiments is carried out, the mating of white and brown mice will produce not spotted or brownish white mice but white mice predominantly. But if this first generation of white mice are mated among themselves, the offspring are not all white but a mixture of pure white and pure brown in the proportion of three whites to one brown. The point this illustrates is that white is a dominant characteristic which shows up in the first generation. However, even though the first generation appears pure white, it has a hidden brown factor which is transmissible to the next generation. But this brown factor is weak as shown by the fact that only one in four of the second generation is brown in colour.

In man a similar case is evident when an albino marries a person with normal pigmentation. The offspring are normal outwardly, but when they marry other apparently normal offspring of normal and albino parents, one out of four of the second generation is albino. Thus the albino parent is recessive. If, on the other hand, an albino marries an albino, then all offspring are albinos. The recessive factors are not inhibited by any dominant factors and show up every time.

17

While Mendel's Law applies in most instances, it is by no means universal. Where both parents have dominant but opposing characteristics, a blending does occur. Certain strains entirely different from those of both parents may appear in the offspring. But these cases are few and far between.

All these examples deal only with single characteristics. But animals as well as men inherit a whole range of traits and characteristics from their parents. The question is how much of the parents' characteristics are hereditary? And above all, how much of the less tangible characteristics such as intelligence, diligence, resourcefulness etc., are inherited? As dominant characteristics are not confined to only one of the parents, it is apparent that the offspring will inherit the dominant characteristics of both parents. Again when both parents have the same recessive factors these will be passed on to the offspring.

In the evolution of a family, hereditary factors play an important part. It is clear that marriage between a couple with good dominant characteristics will produce better offspring, and that when a couple with recessive, bad characteristics are married, the offspring will be recessive. On the other hand, marriage between a person with good dominant characteristics and a person with recessive characteristics will produce a large proportion of offspring with the good characteristics.

A dominant characteristic tends to cancel a recessive characteristic, and it is clear that if the parents have different sets of dominant characteristics, then the offspring will have a combination of all the dominant characteristics of the parents. It follows therefore that the best offspring are those resulting from parents with different good dominant characteristics. Thus since close relatives tend to resemble each other and the chances of carrying similar recessive characteristics are greater, marriage between such relatives will not produce the best offspring. On the other hand, as unrelated people have more differences in characteristics, a marriage between such people would tend to produce ideal offspring with the good dominant characteristics of both parents, while the recessive characteristics are cancelled.

How does environment affect the development of a race and its evolution? Again it is necessary to study a single family before observing a whole race. It is common knowledge that man learns by experience, and that the more the experience the greater is the sum total of his knowledge. It is also common knowledge that man adapts himself to his surroundings. But of far greater importance is man's ability to learn from the experience of others and to copy their example. All these things may be done unconsciously, but they may also be learned consciously. As time goes on, conscious learning overtakes intuitive learning except in the most basic things. To-day, man's opportunity to learn is almost unlimited, but an individual's capacity to learn has varying limitations. There are obviously people who can absorb more knowledge than others. And this difference appears to be an inherent characteristic.

Man's environment must therefore play a great part in shaping him, his family and his race. Next to heredity, environment is the most important factor responsible for the physical, mental, and psychological development of man. Darwin's theory, explained in his *Origin of the Species* may be unacceptable for many reasons, but some of his arguments are nevertheless valid. Applied to man at a later stage in his development the theory seems logical. The world is undoubtedly a dangerous place to live in. From ancient times, death and destruction have lurked in every corner. A sting from an insect can be as good a killer as an atom bomb. The man who survives is the man who knows how to avoid danger. And the man who can avoid all danger must of necessity be cunning and resourceful. The careless and the stupid will fall along the way.

As characteristics are transmissible generationally, it follows that man must become constantly cleverer and more adaptable to his surroundings. This process of adaptation goes on through generations, and in each generation those few incapable of surviving in their environment will be eliminated and deprived of the chance to procreate. The

19

process of weeding out the weak in mind and body goes on until a breed is found sufficiently clever not merely in adapting itself to its surroundings, but also in adapting the surroundings to its needs. Thus, from seeking shelter in caves, man goes on to build his own shelter, and through the ages his simple shelter has grown into the complexes that now form our modern cities.

The effects of heredity and environment on man are inter-related and complementary to each other. The development of a human family and of a race must progress along a line determined by environment and by the transmission of the characteristics of parents to offspring in the families which environment permits to reproduce. The complexity of man's environment however makes it difficult for a short, casual study of this nature to be comprehensive. A man's environment is made up of numerous factors, and usually the effects of one set of conditions are counter-balanced by another. To be methodical it is necessary to take the major constituents of environment one at a time. But it is equally necessary to remember that these constituents are often closely related and interdependent. If we want to examine the development of the Malays in Malaya we must first study the geography of Malaya and deduce its effects on them.

Malaya is a peninsula with numerous rivers and a backbone of mountain ranges flanked by flat, marshy land. The earliest Malay settlers in Malaya must have found the plains extending from the foothills of the central range to the shores of the sea both fertile and easily accessible by river. Food could be found and could be grown in plenty on these plains, and fish and meat must have been easy to come by. The highlands on the other hand were inaccessible, thickly jungled and fraught with danger from prowling wild beasts. Cultivation was difficult, if not impossible, in the highlands. Besides, with so much fertile plain available there was no need to live in the hills and mountains. Hence the Malays became primarily plainsmen, cultivators and fishermen. They lived on the banks of rivers, cultivating the plains extending from the rivers, and moving ever nearer to the foothills. The rivers were their principal means of communication, their source of fish and also their sewerage system. And from one river mouth to another the Malays travelled by sea. Their principal towns were located at river mouths or at the confluence of big rivers.

We know from historical findings that the first major Malay settlements were in the plains of Kedah and other northern or north-eastern states. The southern, more hilly parts of the peninsula were relatively uninhabited until the Sumatrans and the Javanese crossed over to Malaya to found new colonies. Even then these settlements were found in the few small plains which were suitable for rice growing. Later on, the sea which was the means of communication between settlements became also the means of bringing firstly foreign traders, then immigrants, and finally conquerors to Malaya.

Thus geographical considerations have made the Malays people of the lowlands. There was plenty of land for everyone and the hills were never necessary for cultivation or permanent settlement. The lush tropical plains with their plentiful sources of food were able to support the relatively small number of inhabitants of early Malaya. No great exertion or ingenuity was required to obtain food. There was plenty for everyone throughout the year. Hunger and starvation, a common feature in countries like China, were unknown in Malaya. Under these conditions everyone survived. Even the weakest and the least diligent were able to live in comparative comfort, to marry and procreate. The observation that only the fittest would survive did not apply, for the abundance of food supported the existence of even the weakest.

Rice cultivation, in which the majority of the Malays were occupied, is a seasonal occupation. Actual work takes up only two months, but the yield is sufficient for the whole year. This was especially so in the days when the population was small and land was plentiful. There was a lot of free time. Even after the gathering of other food-stuffs, there was still a lot of leisure time left. The hot, humid climate of the land was not conducive to either vigorous work or even to mental activity. Thus, except for a few, people were content to spend their unlimited leisure in merely resting or in extensive conversation with neighbours and friends.

Farming does not lead to the establishment of large communities. Thus the Malays tended to live in small villages or on individual farms. Social contact was limited and so the development of community services was insignificant. Division of labour and specialization of skills were limited as most farmers could provide for their own basic needs. But while the majority of Malays were farmers and lived on the fertile plains, little townships did spring up at the confluence of rivers or at river mouths where fishing and petty trading were carried out. The biggest of these towns were those where the local chiefs or rajas lived.

As can be expected, the people of even these tiny towns were more sophisticated and better organized than the farmers. Patronized by the rajas, craftsmen, scholars, traders and administrators gathered in closer-knit communities which differed more and more from the plainsmen farmers who formed the bulk of the Malay population. Intercourse between the towns and the farming peoples was limited and there was little intermarriage.

Whereas animism was the indigenous religion of the Malays, Hinduism and Islam were foreign in origin. These religions came with the Indian and Arab traders who not only traded, but also settled in the towns and married into the well-established Malay families in these towns. In time these mixed families became rich and very influential. The social and economic differences between the town and the country became more marked. The townsfolk set a pace which the country folk found increasingly difficult to emulate.

The influence of Islam on the Malays was tremendous. The Arabic language and culture which are part and parcel of Islam were absorbed by the Malays and caused drastic changes in their way of life. Adaptation of the Arabic script by Malay scholars resulted in increased literacy and an easier acquisition of the philosophy and sciences of the Middle East. Unfortunately, all the cultural and educational changes brought about by Islam remained for the most part

22

in the town areas. Later on, when teachers moved into, and established religious schools in the rural areas, their teaching was limited to religion only. Philosophy and the sciences did not find ready acceptance. The influence of custom or *adat* and the strong animist beliefs of the rural areas limited Islamic teachings, and caused the practice of Islam to merge with Malay *adat* and its animist basis.

The sophistication of the towns continued to become more and more marked in relation to the rural areas. A high degree of literacy was found in the towns where a certain degree of internationalism prevailed owing to the absorption of immigrant culture and religion, and also to intermarriage.

The adoption of Islam as the religion of the Malays also resulted in the development of a permanent barrier against further changes in religion. Hitherto, Malays had felt free to marry outside their religion. Now Islam forbade such marriage except when certain conditions were met. The stigma attached to those who disregarded religious injunctions was so great that everything which differed from established Islamic practice became suspect and was rejected.

The prosperity of the Malacca Sultanate came at a time when Islam was in the ascendancy in Malaya. Malacca attracted more foreign traders and eventually conquerors and settlers. But, by the time this had happened, the Malays had already become impervious to non-Islamic influence. Thus Chinese immigrants who settled first in Malacca, and then in other parts of Malaya, were completely cut off from the Malays. Whereas in Siam the Chinese were partly absorbed, in Malaya they remained distinct. Even when the Chinese adopted the language, dress and part of the customs of the Malays, they were not acceptable because of religious differences. Intermarriage between Malays and Chinese was extremely rare.

Next to Islam the single most important change in the Malay environment was the massive influx of Chinese immigrants. Until the coming of the Chinese, the Malays of pure or mixed blood were not only the peasants, but also the petty traders, craftsmen, skilled workers, and, through

23

the system of *penghulus* and rajas, the administrators in Malaya. The effect of Chinese immigration on the Malays was conflict between two contrasting racial groups which resulted from two entirely different sets of hereditary and environmental influences. To understand this difference it is necessary to briefly consider the background of the Chinese immigrants.

The history of China is littered with disasters, both natural and man-made. Four thousand years ago a great flood was recorded, and subsequently floods alternated with famine, while waves of invaders, predatory emperors and warlords ravaged the country. For the Chinese people life was one continuous struggle for survival. In the process the weak in mind and body lost out to the strong and the resourceful. For generation after generation, through four thousand years or more, this weeding out of the unfit went on, aided and abetted by the consequent limitation of survival to the fit only. But, as if this was not enough to produce a hardy race, Chinese custom decreed that marriage should not be within the same clan. This resulted in more cross-breeding than in-breeding, in direct contrast to the Malay partiality towards in-breeding. The result of this Chinese custom was to reproduce the best strains and characteristics which facilitated survival and accentuated the influence of environment on the Chinese.

Besides natural catastrophes and repeated wars, the Chinese had to put up with emperors and warlords with their hordes of predatory officials. Again, in order to live and prosper, an ability to placate officials was necessary. The Chinese became so adept at this that the symbiotic relationship between the ordinary citizen and officials became an inherent characteristic of Chinese society. The officials protected the source of their sustenance as much from necessity as from duty. From this it required but a step to move on to the secret society method of affording protection. By the time the Chinese began to emigrate in numbers to the islands and peninsula of Southeast Asia, the effect of environment, heredity and other factors had already had their maximum effect. The people who left the shores of China to seek their fortune abroad were hardened and resourceful. Like emigrants everywhere they were the people who were not content with their lot and were moved by a desire for a better life, and obviously by the determination to work for this. The Chinese who flooded Malaya with the subsequent encouragement of the British were therefore adventurous and resourceful.

The Malays whose own hereditary and environmental influence had been so debilitating, could do nothing but retreat before the onslaught of the Chinese immigrants. Whatever the Malays could do, the Chinese could do better and more cheaply. Before long the industrious and determined immigrants had displaced the Malays in petty trading and all branches of skilled work. As their wealth increased, so did their circle of contacts. Calling on their previous experience with officialdom in their own homeland, the Chinese immigrants were soon establishing the type of relationship between officials and traders which existed in China.

The organized open gratification of the ruling class soon firmly entrenched the Chinese in the towns and helped them establish complete control of the economy. The towns changed in character. The small Malay shops gave way to rows of Chinese shops. As the Chinese increased in number and their business activities expanded, land prices in the town rocketed. Tempted by the high prices offered for their land, the Malays sold their holdings and began moving further and further into the outskirts of the towns. This pattern was already set when the British started their rule. The British at once recognized Chinese enterprise, and realized that a rich Chinese population would be good for British trade. The Chinese not only provided the infrastructure for the proper functioning of the big British import-export houses, but the wealth that they so readily acquired also made them good customers of the British. Chinese immigration was encouraged, and soon the towns began to assume the characteristics of the Malayan towns of today.

Preoccupied with making as much money as they could in as short a time as possible, and still thinking of going back to China after making their fortune, the Chinese saw little future in working as administrators. They left the ruling of the country to the Malays although they resented Malay authority. It may be that the Malays realized early the importance of retaining political control. But had the Chinese decided to take a keener interest in politics in the early days of the British administration, the position of the Malays would have been worse than it is today. As it was, the Malays in the towns were almost exclusively petty officials, and those close to the courts of the rajas. These few Malays became sophisticated, educated and open-minded through contact with foreign races. They also became good administrators and civil servants. A certain amount of intermarriage took place between town Malays and immigrant Indian Muslims and Arabs.

The differences between town Malays and the *kampong* Malays became even more emphasized. The Malays of the rural areas remained purebred. Socially they mixed hardly at all with non-Malays, and were exclusively farmers with no interest in trade or craftsmanship. Deeply religious, orthodox Muslims, the Malays nevertheless remained in abiding fear of the evil spirits of their past animist beliefs. The town Malays were usually of mixed Malay-Indian or Malay-Arab descent. They moved freely among non-Malay Muslims. They had been ousted from business by the Chinese, but had made progress as officials and administrators. Although they were good Muslims, they were more tolerant of other religions, and to a large extent they had rejected their animist past. The influence of Hinduism was still strong and showed in their marriage and other customs. The setting was thus perfect for the divide and rule policy of the British which was to lead to the almost complete elimination of the Malays as the rulers of the country.

The British did not merely divide the Malays from the Chinese, but went on to divide the rural Malays from the town Malays. It is true that the division was already there, but it was British policy which very neatly severed the tenuous links that the town Malays had with the rural Malays. The process of division was subtle. It took advantage

26

of everything that already existed and also of some new creations of the British. Both the division from the Chinese and the division between rural and town Malays affected the character of the Malays considerably, and rendered them more and more impotent politically and economically.

Seeing how the Chinese had destroyed the self-reliance of the Malays in craftsmanship, skilled work and business, the British encouraged Chinese immigration until the Malays were completely excluded from these fields of employment. The town Malays however were encouraged to retain their hold on administration. By then they had realized that the Chinese could be a menace, and they appreciated British support of their desire to retain some semblance of political authority. But a political authority entrusted to a solid Malay nation would be dangerous to the British. Taking advantage of the existing lack of cohesion between town and country Malays, the British created further conditions to keep them apart. Having encouraged white collar jobs among town Malays, they made these people feel that their status was above that of manual workers and peasants.

The few Malays who remained in the town were then provided with an elementary English education which was at the same time denied the rural Malays. The system of land reservation for the Malays physically assisted the division. Malays from the rural areas found it difficult to acquire town land which was usually unreserved. Rural land almost completely reserved for Malays ensured that Malay development and expansion would remain rural. Provisions for the excision of Malay reserved land further enabled the British to move the Malays in any direction they wanted while retaining the impression that they were anxious to protect the Malays from the predatory Chinese.

Communication between rural Malays and town Malays was further hindered by lack of roads. The roads built by the British linked only the towns and were merely sufficient for administrative purposes and for the exportation of rubber and tin. Education remained at a low level, and news could not be disseminated freely in the rural areas. No real attempt was made to improve the earning capacity of the

27

farmers. Finally, the health of the rural people was completely neglected. Malaya abounded with various debilitating, endemic diseases like malaria and yaws. In addition, small epidemics of cholera and dysentery occurred at regular intervals. As often happens to a community subjected to continuous exposure to these diseases, the rural Malays developed a certain amount of resistance. They survived, but all their energy was depleted. Malaria, for example, affected practically all rural Malays. Rendered weak and dull by lack of blood and frequent bouts of fever, they were disinclined to work more than was necessary, The effort to plant and reap padi, which occupied two months of every year, taxed their strength. They had no more energy left to earn a better livelihood, or to teach themselves new skills.

The other diseases had a similar effect on the activities of the *kampong* dwellers. Their will to progress, never great because of lack of contact with the outside world, became negligible. Soon they were left behind in all fields. The rest of the world went by, and the tremendous changes of the late nineteenth and twentieth centuries took place without the rural Malays being even spectators. In the meantime the town Malays benefited somewhat from the changes going on round them. They became better educated, more sophisticated from mixing with other communities and from the changes going on in the world, and they had better health. Newspapers, postal and other communication services, and travel gave them a wider horizon.

The character of the town Malays became more diverse and they found no difficulty in changing with the times. Some intermarried. An important aspect of intra-religious intermarriages worth noting is that, no matter whether the father or the mother was Malay, the offspring invariably considers himself Malay. These intermarriages enriched Malay stock. Of course not all town Malays married non-Malays, but as time went on, town Malays inherited a certain amount of mixed blood as more and more offspring of intermarriages became indistinguishable from the Malays themselves, and married as Malays.

The absence of inter-racial marriages in the rural areas resulted in purebred Malays. This was further aggravated by the habit of family in-breeding. Malays, especially rural Malays, prefer to marry relatives. First cousin marriages were and still are frequent, and the result is the propagation of the poorer characteristics, whether dominant or recessive, originally found in the brothers or sisters who were parents of the married couple.

Another factor that affected the physiological development of the Malays, again especially in the rural areas, was the habit of marrying early. It was, and still is, common to see married couples of thirteen or fourteen. These early marriages mean reproduction takes place before full maturity of the parents. The effects on both parents and children are well known. Perhaps the most deleterious effect is that the parents are not ready to take care of the children. The parents in fact remain dependent on their own parents who, exulting in their early attainment of the status of grandparents, happily undertake the care of their children's children as well. In this sort of society, enterprise and independence are unknown. The upbringing of children is distorted by the well-known excessive indulgence of grandparents and the incapacity of the parents to take care of the children. The long term effect on community and race is disastrous.

Malays abhor the state of celibacy. To remain unmarried was and is considered shameful. Everyone must be married at some time or other. The result is that whether a person is fit or unfit for marriage, he or she still marries and reproduces. An idiot or a simpleton is often married off to an old widower, ostensibly to take care of him in his old age. If this is not possible, backward relatives are paired off in marriage. These people survive, reproduce and propagate their species. The cumulative effect of this can be left to the imagination.

Although not truly affecting hereditary characteristics, the health of the parents plays a great part in the development of the children. We know how malaria and other diseases affect the physical and mental energy of the rural

Malays. When parents, and especially mothers, are continuously afflicted by these diseases, the care of children becomes neglected. As a result, Malay children grow up ill-prepared to face the challenge of living in competition and confrontation with the aggressive immigrant races.

Since World War II the environment of the Malays has changed repeatedly and radically. The Japanese Occupation had a profound effect on the Malays. Their faith in the invincibility of the British was destroyed. War and the Japanese Occupation brought hardships that were unfamiliar. The Malays were forced out of their complacent reliance on others. To survive, the Malays had to struggle for almost the first time. For many, however, there was a comfortable feeling that everything would be all right again once the British returned. But they were in for a rude awakening. The British came back but not in the role the Malays had cast for them. They came back not as the protectors of the Malays they used to be, but showed instead every intention to wrest everything away from the Malays.

Under the stress of this rapid destruction of their hopes, the Malay character underwent a metamorphosis. Seeing their salvation in politics, the previously docile Malays, with remarkable rapidity and initiative, organized themselves. Malay leaders sprang up almost from nowhere, and political topics which had hitherto only interested a few of the elite became common subjects for discussion and debate everywhere. An aggressive spirit pervaded Malay society at all levels and this same spirit carried the Malays through to *merdeka*.

The Malays who achieved *merdeka* were not by character quite the same Malays who had allowed the British to overrun their country and displace them with Chinese and Indians. Circumstances leading to *merdeka* had forced a different outlook on life in general, a different attitude to surroundings and a different way of approaching and tackling the problems that faced the Malays. For a time it seemed as if they would really break away from their lethargic, self-effacing past. But it would seem on closer examination that all these changes were superficial. Deep under, the inherent traits and character acquired over the centuries persist.

Merdeka brought power and wealth to the new Malay *elite*. The trials and tribulations of the war and immediate post-war years were over. Politics was found to be the panacea. It provided a short-cut to everything. It made possible the attainment of positions of immense power. It brought about laws and policies that placed some Malays in a position to acquire great wealth, or at least a good livelihood without trying too hard. It made life in the *kampongs* more comfortable and less isolated from the towns. In other words, politics created for the Malays a soft environment which removed all challenge to their survival and progress.

The question that arises now is how will heredity and this new environment affect the Malays? We can expect that the new environment will not be good for the Malays. They will become softer and less able to overcome difficulties on their own. Because of this, political power might ultimately prove their complete downfall.

But the alternative is equally without promise. Removal of all protection would subject the Malays to the primitive laws that enable only the fittest to survive. If this is done it would perhaps be possible to breed a hardy and resourceful race capable of competing against all comers. Unfortunately, we do not have four thousand years to play around with.

Besides, unlike China which had no considerable immigrant settlers, Malaysia has far too many non-Malay citizens who can swamp the Malays the moment protection is removed. The frequent suggestion that the only way to help the Malays is to let them fight their own battles cannot therefore be seriously considered. The answer seems to lie somewhere in between; in a sort of "constructive protection" worked out after a careful study of the effects of heredity and environment. Until this is done, the deleterious effect of heredity and environment on the Malays is likely to continue.

4: The Malay Economic Dilemma

In this chapter I have attempted to trace and sometimes deduce the economic history of the Malays during the different periods of Malayan history in order to provide a background for present-day conditions.

The Malay view of his inferior economic position is described with as much objectivity as a Malay could muster. The faults of the Malays are not overlooked but it would be wrong not to take others to task for their methods and attitudes. What is clear is that unless the Chinese in particular are willing to hold themselves back and appreciate the need to bring the Malays up in the economic field, not even the determination of the Malays and the schemes of the Government can help to solve the Malay economic dilemma.

It is now almost impossible to imagine a Malaysia without the ubiquitous Chinese shopkeeper. They perform a function that has become so much a part of Malaysian life that it must seem to everyone that they have been there since the beginning of time. They are the universal middlemen. They not only sell the whole country the necessities of life and the luxuries, but they often buy up the produce of their customers and dispose of it elsewhere. They are an important and essential cog in the machinery of the Malaysian economy.

Yet we know that at one time they were not there. In the history of the Malay sultanates of Kedah, Kelantan and Malacca there was a period when the Chinese shopkeepers were absent. These sultanates were then already organized societies with distinct urban and rural communities, and with internal and external trade. The marketing of produce, transportation and the buying and selling of goods imported or manufactured locally went on without the so-called indispensable Chinese shopkeepers. It may be that the efficiency and enterprise of the Chinese were absent, but the states were organized for commerce, primitive and limited though it must have been.

Between this period of Malay economic independence and the present, a whole series of events took place which precipitated the economic dilemma that the Malays are in today.

There is little doubt that Malays were exclusively involved in marketing, petty trading, importing and exporting and even manufacturing in the early Malay sultanates. There were skilled Malay craftsmen, artisans and skilled labourers. Except for a much smaller population and a more limited area, economic life went on very much the way it now goes on despite the fact that there were no Chinese.

The early Malay towns were settlements at the confluence of rivers and their estuaries. The reason for this choice is obvious as the rivers and the seas were the main means of communication. Horses and horse-drawn carriages were almost unknown, and road transport was mainly by elephants or bullock-carts. The locations of the towns facilitated travel and communication. When man travels, commerce involving bartering and some form of monetary token become necessary. The traveller cannot possibly sustain himself without buying at least some of his necessities.

The Malay towns were essentially market towns, each administered by a chief. In the largest town, usually a port, lived the Malay raja. The court of the raja and the administrators required both goods and services. Under these conditions organized commerce emerged and flourished.

By the time the Indians and the Arabs came to Malaya, the sultanates were already quite well-developed in commerce and industry, and had the facilities and the personnel for the import and export business that followed. Evidence shows that the rajas themselves were involved in business, although in the main what this amounted to was the appropriation of a certain portion of goods belonging to their subjects, and exchanging these for goods brought by foreign merchants. In this way vast amounts of clothing and jewellery were amassed by the rajas and the members of the courts. A proportion of these goods flowed into the local markets enabling even ordinary subjects to exchange their goods for foreign goods.

Money means sophistication in business. We do not know exactly when money in the form of coins was first used in Malaya. What we do know is that it antedated the coming of the Chinese. Ancient Malay coins show strong evidence of Indian and Arab influence and very little, if any at all, Chinese influence. It follows that sophisticated commerce involving money instead of barter was already in progress when the Chinese came.

The Indians and the Arabs changed the pattern of trade in the old Malay sultanates. They not only traded, but some of them settled and married Malays close to the courts of the rajas. Because these merchants had to be astute in business and reasonably rich in order to trade so far from their homeland, it is not surprising that their abilities were soon recognized and utilized by the Malay rajas. They became very influential in the Malay courts and were in time accepted as Malays. Quite naturally they became more and more involved in the commercial life of the country, but they were regarded even by themselves not as foreigners but as Malays. Their business know-how and their contacts with the courts as well as with foreign merchants brought a new sophistication into Malay business. No longer were the rajas required to trade directly. Henceforth they, as well as the *ra'ayat,* were serviced by competent merchants and shopkeepers, whom they could still identify with their own race, even though the racial origins were different.

During these changes, the Chinese merchants began to arrive, to trade and to settle in limited numbers. In the Malacca Sultanate the inflow was small at first. The monsoon winds which permitted sailings between Malacca and China only during certain seasons meant that the Chinese traders had to stop in Malacca for a fairly considerable length of time. It does not take much imagination to understand how this led to the stationing of trading personnel between seasons.

At first the Chinese merely acted as agents for their own countrymen, selling goods from China and buying up local produce for export to China. But their sophistication in business brought them riches and influence. They in turn became useful and convenient to the rajas because of their trade, and they brought new importance and wealth to the country. Their habit of giving expensive gifts to the ruling class ingratiated them with all levels of authority in the states. The prejudice against them melted away and in time they found that they could move and do business freely everywhere.

In no time at all even the lowly employees from among the personnel stationed in Malacca began their own businesses with small retail shops. The success of these petty traders led to a greater influx of Chinese small-time merchant-adventurers. Soon the system of retail shops had penetrated every nook and corner of Malaysia, and became an established feature of life in the old Malay sultanates.

The arrival of the Portuguese, the Dutch and finally the British gave this trend the final push. It must be remembered that the Europeans came out East not to conquer but to trade. In the quest of trade, however, they were prepared to do anything. They conquered and they plundered. They made treaties and they broke them. They were in fact completely unscrupulous.

For these unscrupulous people the Chinese traders were a godsend. The Chinese knew the local language and had all the contacts as well as the set up necessary to enable the European traders to milk the Malay sultanates dry. In no time at all, perfect *rapport* was established between the Chinese traders and the conquering merchants of the West. As this partnership grew and as the Chinese partners proved their usefulness over and over again, Chinese migration to Malaysia was encouraged and speeded up. Now there came a bonus for the British who were the successors of the Portuguese and the Dutch in Malaya. The Chinese who grew rich under British protection themselves became good customers of the British. The market for British goods in Malaya enlarged and became very profitable. With the Chinese traders came the skilled workers and finally the unskilled coolies. To the British rulers of the country the influx of Chinese of all grades and classes meant a more sophisticated and organized society which facilitated their business as much as their administration. But for the Malays the influx meant a displacement. First it was in trade and commerce, then in skilled work and finally even in unskilled labour. There was also displacement in location, for the Malays had to move out of the towns, where, unless they were employed by the Government, there was no reason for them to stay. Indeed, the increased value of land in the towns and the various rates and taxes forced them to sell off their holdings and buy cheaper rural land.

Thus the geo-political pattern came to conform with the socio-economic pattern of the country. As time went on the division became more and more marked. The policies of various municipalities and town councils which insisted on well-built brick houses with well laid-out plans and modern facilities helped to eliminate the few Malays who tried to hang on to their miserable pieces of land in the towns. In Kuala Lumpur, a belatedly compassionate municipality decided on a Malay Reserve within the town limits to prevent the Malays from being completely expelled from the city. But elsewhere, especially where British rule was more direct, the Malays found no champion at all.

By the nineteen thirties, the Malays realized that the economic dilemma they were in was of such complexity as to defy solution by them alone. Malay senior Government officers began to cast around for plans to bring Malays back into the economic orbit. But their lack of authority and their subservience to the British limited their efforts. What materialized were tiny weekly fairs, as in Kedah, where Malays were given the exclusive rights to sell jungle produce and simple daily necessities. If anything, these markets served to further spotlight and emphasize their economic dilemma.

The Japanese occupation marked yet another phase of this dilemma. With the defeat of the British, thousands of Malays who had found security in Government employment in the urban areas, lost their jobs when the Japanese retrenched Government staff. Suddenly it became necessary for these white-collar workers to involve themselves in hawking and peddling in order to keep body and soul together.. And just as suddenly they realized what other thinking Malays had realized just before the war — that the economic dilemma of the Malays was hopeless and complete.

With this realization came not determination, but lassitude, and a wish to return to the humdrum life and security of employment under the British. The whole episode which plunged them into the far from sedate life of petty traders was regarded as temporary. For most there was no wish to overcome the resistance of the Chinese in business and to break their monopoly. But inevitably a few worked up sufficient resentment over their exclusion from commerce to wish to alter the state of affairs then existing.

Thus it was that when the war ended and the British returned, there was a definite move among a small section of the Malays to use the political power which they expected to regain in order to penetrate the business world. But the British shocked the Malays with their Malayan Union proposal, and for a time the Malay economic plight became subservient to the more urgent political problems.

But as soon as some semblance of Malay political power returned, attention was once again focused on their exclusion from the commercial life of the country. The rehabilitation of Chinese business activities disrupted by inflation, a scarcity of goods and the monopolistic practice of the Japanese during the occupation, was rapid. Starting with widespread black-market deals and a multitude of contracts with the British Military Administration, the impoverished Chinese traders soon gathered sufficient capital to re-establish their old businesses.

The Malays found the confused unorthodox deals which characterized the early years after the war beyond their limited business knowledge. Not adept at bribery and manipulation, and deserted by the better educated who had returned to Government service, the opportunity of getting rich quick, and making a place for themselves was lost. When the dust settled and the British Military Administration bowed out, the Malays once again realized that they had to face the same old pattern in which the Chinese controlled all business that was not big enough for the big British business houses.

Nevertheless, the Malays made sporadic attempts to enter the business world. Public companies were floated, went through the formalities of inaugural meetings and appointments of directors and other officers, and then foundered on the rocks of inexperience and the massive resistance of the established non-Malay enterprises. The small capital in the hands of the Malays was dissipated, and a loss of faith in company promoters prevented subscription to new ventures.

Then the idea of a bank as a source of capital captured Malay imagination. But for two or three local Chinese banks, all banks in Malaya then were under British control. All these banks refused to have anything to do with Malay business. Perhaps they were justified, but justified or not, the Malays resented this solid bar to their entry into business in their own country.

Thus it was that a Malay National Bank was proposed amidst opposition from a fairly considerable number of orthodox Malays who felt the practice of interest collection in banking business was against Muslim teaching. Despite this, a number of prominent Malays gave their moral and material support to the bank. A fairly considerable sum of money was collected, and the bank started business with more nationalist ideals than business acumen.

The end came with startling drama and finality. During its existence the bank was never much of a help to the Malays, but its decease left them feeling more vulnerable than ever in the jungle of Malayan business. Their resentment sharpened against all the forces that not only thwarted them in their attempts to solve their dilemma but also gloated over their futile fumblings.

The gloom that descended on the Malays with the failure of their bank was reflected in their political attitude to other races and to the British administration. It is to the credit of the British that they sensed this feeling of frustration while others remained completely insensitive to it.

But to the British this frustration only meant that conditions were right for more bargaining over the political future of the country. At about this time the Sino-Malay relationship was going through one of its periodic crises. Under UMNO the Malays insisted on a Malaya for the Malays. On the other hand the Chinese demanded citizenship by right of birth.

Efforts were made by the Commissioner-General for Southeast Asia to bring the two races together through the Communities Liaison Committee, but although the leaders were persuaded, the rank and file remained stubborn. The Malays were not going to give way despite talks of Sino-Malay brotherhood. They knew too well the economic stranglehold that the Chinese held in Malaya. They reasoned that if to this was added political power, the Malays would be completely helpless and at the mercy of the Chinese. They had no reason to believe that understanding and sympathy was a strong Chinese trait.

It was at this juncture that the High Commissioner came up with the proposal to create the now much criticized Rural and Industrial Development Authority. The Malays were told that they would get Government aid in solving their economic dilemma provided they were more accommodating politically. A sum of five million dollars was to be allocated to a new development authority which would help develop Malay cottage industries and aid Malays in business by providing capital and know-how.

This was something completely new in terms of Government policy. Government aid for business was quite unknown. It is true that British firms, local and England-based, were favoured by the Government, but this was not a stated policy. Usually this help took the form of large contracts negotiated not officially but over whiskies in the various exclusive clubs in the country. For the Malays in particular, Government aid was actually negative. Any Malay wanting to do business with the Government, or to start a major enterprise like mining or transport, was invariably asked whether he had any experience. As his exclusion from the business world by the British and the Chinese was complete, the only answer he could give to this inevitable query was negative. His inexperience was then taken as an excuse not to give him any licence or contract, and so permanently to deny him any experience.

It is understandable that the Malays were attracted by this idea of a Rural and Industrial Development Authority to help them in business. Their lament had always been lack of capital. Their bank had failed. And now the British were actually proposing to use Government money as capital for them, and as a bonus they were actually to be given business guidance by the Government. The father image of the British received a massive boost. Could people who thought up such a benevolent and liberal idea be anything but sincere and just?

But, as if all that was not enough, the British indicated that the Malays would administer the fund themselves through one of their own political leaders. The five million dollars were to be their very own. All they had to do to lay their hands on the money was to be broadminded and to cooperate. In any case, once they had a firm grip on the country's economy, they need not fear Chinese political encroachment so much.

What happened with RIDA is now history. Run on the lines of a welfare department, RIDA denied money to capable Malay businessmen but gave hand-outs to poor people with vague notions of going into business. Anyone with any indication at all of succeeding in business was denied aid on the grounds that RIDA was not meant to help rich people become richer. Indeed, in some instances RIDA ensured that where these fairly successful Malay businessmen had no competition, they now would have competition from RIDA-financed Malays whose business methods were calculated to destroy everything.

It is true that there were instances where RIDA succeeded. But in the main this was merely in subsidising businesses which made possible competition with non-Malays. Other fields in which the Authority was successful were not so much business as education. RIDA enabled a lot of Malays to get an education which fitted them for work in commercial houses, instead of leaving them entirely dependent on Government employment.

But by and large RIDA did not fulfill the promise that the British made. Having allotted the money and chosen the Malays to administer this economic panacea, the British backed out completely. Now they were free once again to swill their whiskies in their clubs and give more contracts to British firms. If the Malays showed little improvement with RIDA, well it was their fault. In any case, what the British wanted through RIDA was not Malay economic rehabilitation, but something else entirely. And this the British got when the Malays agreed to cooperate with the Chinese and facilitate the prosecution of the Emergency.

RIDA may not have succeeded as much as it should, but it did a lot in changing the thinking of Malays in the economic activities of the country. It banished once and for all the idea that the Government has no obligation to help improve the lot of the Malays in business. Henceforth every Malay venture, even if it expects no Government aid, can at least insist that the Government does not obstruct it on grounds of inexperience, lack of capital and a variety of other irrelevant excuses. RIDA also impressed on the non-Malays, especially the Chinese, that neither the Malays nor the Government were going to accept as a matter of course the exclusion of the Malays from the commercial life of the country.

Once the principle that helping the Malays is not racialism but is actually essential for the stability of the country was accepted, various other agencies and methods were initiated by the Malays and the Government to take advantage of this change in attitude. For example, the grossly unfair provision by which Malay Reserve Land rich in tin or other minerals could be excised and substituted with less valuable jungle was no longer invoked without first letting the Malays know of the intention. As expected, this small change in policy alone saved the Malays millions of dollars.

Government even insisted that a certain percentage of employees in new industries must be Malay. Valuable land in the urban areas belonging to the state are no longer sold

41

only to the highest bidder or to the astute Chinese or Europeans who are quicker to realize their value and more able to use them. Malays are given the chance to buy the land at prices which are within their means, or at least to pay in instalments over a reasonable period of time. State Governments also feel that they have a responsibility to lend whatever help is necessary for Malay participation in commerce. Malay Chambers of Commerce are for the first time regarded as the voice of Malay businessmen even if their members are no more than hawkers and itinerant peddlers.

While these changes in ideas and values were taking place, Malaya gained independence. It is no exaggeration to say that it was the Malays who most wanted independence. They knew that a Government in which they had a greater say would be more liberal in aiding them in commerce as well as in other fields. The Chinese business tycoons saw this as well. They saw the end of the days when they could have the exclusive rights to whatever the British chose to leave behind in the business field. They saw an end to the evasions and manipulations that had in the past made a mockery of every law to protect the Malays. They foresaw an invasion of their business empire. Some even had gloomy visions of a Malay socialist state in which all the wealth amassed by them would be expropriated.

In the event, few of the expectations of the Malays were fulfilled. But what is more amazing, not only were the fears of the Chinese tycoons proved to be unjustified, but independent Malaya actually opened up for them more and better avenues for the acquisition of unlimited wealth.

We have already spoken of the increased help the Malays received from the Government as a result of the change in ideas which the formation of RIDA helped to initiate. Needless to say the achievement of independence boosted this trend. The various agencies and schemes of the Federal and State Governments, such as the State Development Boards, and quotas in the road transport business, were the direct result of Independence. It must be admitted that the post-Independence government did, and still does make every effort to help Malays in business. Sometimes graft defeats the object of the Government. Sometimes strangulation by established Chinese business tie-ups achieves the same effect. But despite all this, the favoured position of the Malays has caused a minute dent in the armour of non-Malay economic hegemony. Rightly or wrongly, Malays cannot any longer be entirely ignored in the business world. One of the results of the independent Government's policy is the appointment of Malays as directors in large non-Malay companies.

Everyone knows that more often than not these Malay directors have neither a single cent invested, nor probably have they the personal capacity to contribute to the all-important job of making profits for the company. Everyone knows that some of these Malays are merely selling their names and taking advantage of the policies of a government which wants to see a more equitable distribution of wealth. Everyone knows that this is not really what the Malays or anyone else want. But everyone also knows that there is no alternative if the Malays are to get acquainted with the nerve centres of big business rapidly, as they must, if the gap between them and the non-Malays is not to be permanent.

Are the critics of these Malays who have lent their names to business ventures completely right? Good or bad, able or incapable, the presence of these Malays on the various boards means that they must at least become familiar with the ways of business. Most of them are not entirely stupid. They definitely have the capacity to learn, and evidence shows that most of them are now sufficiently conversant with business methods to be able to actually impart a lot of know-how to new ventures launched by Malays. Then again, their mere presence on the boards prevents the bias against the Malays in general, and employing Malays in particular, from being as absolute as it was in the past. Because of them, Malays cannot be rejected off-hand as employees, and Malays can actually do business with these firms — something that was almost impossible before.

43

Finally, by virtue of their status, these directors are in a .position to acquire riches. At first this might seem grossly unfair. These few Malays, for they are still only very few, have waxed rich not because of themselves but because of the policy of a Government supported by a huge majority of poor Malays. It would seem that the efforts of the poor Malays have gone to enrich a select few of their own people. The poor Malays themselves have not gained one iota. But if these few Malays are not enriched the poor Malays will not gain either. It is the Chinese who will continue to live in huge houses and regard the Malays as only fit to drive their cars. With the existence of the few rich Malays at least the poor Malays can say that their fate is not entirely to serve the rich non-Malays. From the point of view of racial ego, and this ego is still strong, the unseemly existence of Malay tycoons is essential.

As a bonus, these rich Malays have become a source of capital and leadership in business, a status which the Malays previously lacked. Because of their position, these people can have access not only to the various business set-ups in this country, but also to various Government departments whose officers were wont to turn up their noses at aspiring Malay businessmen. The money which they have acquired has become an asset to the Malays as a whole because by and large, these Malays do have a sense of obligation to their country and their people. Besides, in cases where the Government indicates that it intends to favour Malay enterprise, it is these wealthy Malays who must be relied upon to contribute whatever capital and know-how that may be found among the Malay community. Without them the new attitude of the Government towards Malay business would come to nothing. The number of Malay business concerns resulting from Government policy and the new availability of Malay capital and know-how has resulted in a greater diffusion of wealth among the Malays.

It can be seen that, after all, the so-called sinecure jobs of the Malay directors of non-Malay firms are of some value to the economic well-being of the Malays as a whole. In a small and indirect way they have contributed towards changing the pattern of commerce which has been so much in favour of the non-Malays. They have broken into the formerly exclusive circle of big businessmen whose words and deeds could bring wealth or poverty to any class, race or group of people. If this circle is allowed to remain exclusively non-Malay, it could cause such disparity in the distribution of wealth among the different races in this country that civil strife must one day become inevitable. As it is this danger has diminished. The Malay directors have thus performed a function which is nationally important and of some value to the economic position of the Malays. The criticism against them in the absence of any alternative solution is, therefore, unjustified.

Before leaving this subject, it must be pointed out that of late the new Malay company directors are no longer of the same calibre as the first few. As more and more Malay lawyers, accountants, secretaries and doctors go into practice, they form a pool of talent on which the various companies can draw. The new Malay directors are professionally capable and have the ability to develop into efficient and knowledgeable company directors. They do not merely contribute their names but are real assets to the companies they direct. They are also people of some means and so are able to afford some ethics in their dealings with the companies. This means that they have a real say in the running of their companies and are not merely existing by virtue of Government policy.

It might be thought that if these people are a real asset to the companies they work for, then there is no necessity for the Government to encourage their employment by the non-Malay business houses. The fact is that without this policy, Malay talent in business would never be able to manifest itself; and even if it could, the racialist feelings in the business community are so strong that they would employ people of their own race anyhow. The Government is fully justified in adopting a positive policy of encouraging Malay participation in the non-Malay companies in the country.

Apart from the Malay directors, the most criticized

45

by-product of the Government's obligation to help the Malays is the much maligned "Ali-Baba" business set-up. This results from the Government policy of favouring Malays with licences for business. As the number of Malays with capital and know-how is limited, licences for various types of business, especially transportation, must eventually go to those Malays with neither capital nor know-how. The easiest way out for these Malays is to go into partnership with Chinese with capital and know-how. This in itself is quite legitimate and defensible. Unfortunately there is a tendency for the Malay partners to accept a fixed sum for the licences and then have nothing to do with the running of the business. This arrangement is what has come to be known as the "Ali-Baba" business.

This type of arrangement is neither new nor peculiar to the Malays. It happens all the time everywhere. It is well known, for example, that quite a few Chinese who have acquired prospecting licences do no more than arrange with established Chinese miners to prospect and mine on the concessions they have obtained. Their role in the business is confined to collecting royalties. In other types of business too, where licences or permits are necessary, it is a frequent practice to farm out these licences. Indeed, joint-venture pioneer industries where local promoters get the licence and arrange with foreign companies to set up and finance the industry come within the category of licence peddling.

From the point of view of increasing Malay participation in business the "Ali-Baba" arrangement is certainly not to be recommended. However there is no justification for focusing so much attention on this abuse of Malay privileges. Not all Sino-Malay partnerships are "Ali-Baba" affairs. In most instances the role played by the Malay partners is considerable. All dealings with the licence-issuing authorities initially and subsequently must at least be made by them. Apart from this, sheer necessity must throw them into the company of Chinese businessmen. Only a complete imbecile can fail to learn something from this association. In any case in a country where ninety per cent of the wealth is in the hands of the Chinese, it is ridiculous to set up exclusively Malay companies which cater only for the poor Malays. For a business to prosper it must not shut itself off from the Chinese. Being exclusively Malay is one sure way of doing this.

The "Ali-Baba" arrangement will continue to be a feature of Malay participation in business for a long time. This is unfortunate, but the fact that it exists cannot be used as an argument to do away with the preferential treatment which the Malays get in the matter of licences. It is clear that without this preferential treatment, the future of Malay participation in the commercial life of the country would be dark indeed. A time will come when there may not be any need for this treatment, but that time has certainly not arrived yet.

Independence has therefore definitely boosted Malay involvement in the commercial life of the nation. More Malays are working as company directors, transport operators, mine-owners, contractors and petty-traders. In the professional field there is also an increase in the number of Malays. The number of Malay accounting and secretarial firms have increased partly because Government is no longer committed to giving all its business to British firms. Import and export firms have also sprung up, as Malays become more knowledgeable in business and establish their own contacts with foreign firms and agencies. Even the cottage industries on the east coast have increased their volume of business, initially with the interest shown by the Government, and then because of the real merit of their products.

But despite all this progress, the economic dilemma of the Malays still exists. It is there because for every step forward that the Malays make in the economic field other races make ten. It is there because other policies of the independent Government of Malaysia offset the policy towards helping the Malays. It is there because the concept of business has changed and changed again, even as the Malays begin to understand the orthodox methods which had originally defeated them.

There can be no denying that the volume of internal trade has increased by leaps and bounds since the war ended, and has continued to do so with Independence. The yearly trade figures clearly show this. But what the trade figures do not show is the gradual and positive ousting of the established British trading concerns since Independence in terms of proportion of trade, and their replacement by Chinese firms. Under the British regime the Chinese only got what the British did not want for themselves. What the British wanted was considerable. Practically all the import-export houses were British or at least European. These firms were protected by the Government without any need for legislation. The exclusive European clubs throughout the country were the places where these protective "laws" were made and implemented. The firms were assured that what they imported would meet with little or no competition from imports by local firms.

This protection was equally comprehensive on the export side. Markets in rubber and tin for example were established by these firms in their own countries, and the markets were not open to any local firms. The Chinese, whether they had the capacity or not, had to trade through these British and European firms. Their rubber and tin had to be sold to these firms at a price controlled by these firms and to no one else. Knowing that the British Colonial Government was behind these firms, the Chinese made little attempt to establish their own markets or to find their own contracts abroad.

As if Government protection was not enough, the British controlled the whole of the banking business, especially that portion concerned with the financing of the import-export business. These banks dealt with local businessmen very much in the same way as the Government officers dealt with people. Needless to say, the British and European banking officials were also members of the exclusive European clubs and did most of their business there. The exclusion of the Chinese was tacitly agreed upon between the Government officers, the business houses and the financing banks.

Finally the Europeans controlled shipping almost completely. But for small vessels used in trading between Malaya and the then Dutch East Indies, all ships plying between Malaya and other countries had British or other European firms as their agents in Malaya. With this grip on international shipping, the exclusion of the Chinese from the import and export business was complete.

Internally, the Government channelled all substantial contracts for construction or supplies exclusively through British firms. More than now the major construction works and importation of modern equipment into the country were done by the Government. Government contracts for construction or supplies were sufficient to maintain the various firms. So institutionalized was the doling out of contracts to the British firms, that the brass plaques on foundation stones which were put on all Government buildings often carried the name of the British firm or the contractor himself, a practice which is unthinkable today. The quotations for the contracts ensured a margin of profit which was just short of robbery. The local Chinese contractors could hope for only the smallest contracts or for sub-contracts from the British firms whose profits were such that they could give out the whole contract, while still retaining substantial profits.

Contracts for supplies were almost exclusively through the Crown Agents. Local supplies, when required, were by contract with British firms, even if this meant that the firms would have to buy from local Chinese shops. Because British officials and businessmen formed a close-knit community usually presided over by the local British Adviser or Resident, the Chinese could not even bribe their way to the better contracts. The chances of being found out were too great. The almost absolute authority of the British Resident or Adviser over the civil servants meant immediate and effective punishment for the civil servant who was tempted. As for the offending company, it would be black-listed.

The Japanese occupation opened the eyes of the local Chinese businessmen to the huge profits that deals with the

Government could mean. When the war ended the British blithely returned to their old ways. The ever increasing reconstruction undertaken by the Government meant huge contracts for old and new British firms. The resentment of local Chinese business circles could well be imagined. Nibbling at the fringes had whetted their appetite for more, but there was little hope of getting at the tastier morsels as long as the British ruled.

When Malaya became independent, the drive for Malayanization extended into every field. Not only were the expatriate officers in the Government Services Malayanized, but all the old institutions and systems were also Malayanized. And along with this went a change in the policy of protecting and nurturing only British firms. Almost overnight the door was opened for Malayans to have a share in the huge business contracts which the Government ladled out yearly. Construction contracts, supply contracts and a whole string of other profitable Government deals were suddenly thrown at Malaysians as of right. Millions of dollars were there for the taking.

In the mad scramble that followed, the Chinese won hands down. Having more business acumen, capable of improvising at short notice, and backed by newly-founded Chinese banks and their own considerable personal wealth, they were soon organized to replace the established firms. Their business expanded rapidly and tremendously. More money flowed their way and helped further to consolidate their economic grip on the country. Their family ties and the extreme chauvinism which characterized their business practice excluded everyone else from sharing in the bounty. They almost completely replaced the British business circles which used to control Government contracts.

Independent Malaya did not stop at only the Malayanization of jobs and businesses. To keep pace with other countries a policy of development was launched which involved not only massive Government spending but also actual Government financial aid to new enterprises. The partly Government-financed and Government-backed Malaya Borneo Building Society, for example, channelled huge sums of money into housing development. The Malaysia Industrial Development Finance Limited provided capital, know-how and sites for industries which were totally or partially directed by local people. The Rubber Replanting Board made replanting by large estates possible. Exemption from tax for pioneer industries as well as insistence on local capital meant an increase in business opportunities for Malayan citizens.

This greatly increased share in the nation's commercial activities which were opened to Malaysians meant simply that greater wealth accrued to the Chinese. Without British exclusiveness to hamper them, there was nothing to prevent them from completely monopolizing every grade and type of trade and commerce in Malaya. Indeed Malaysian anxiety to Malayanize and Malaysianize meant complete Sinocization of the economy of the country.

It can be seen therefore, that although the Malays have managed to enter the economic field, they have never been able to, and can never hope to catch up with the Chinese. Even as Independence brought the Malays increased opportunities, it has brought the Chinese even greater opportunities which have propelled them so far ahead as to make the entry of the Malays into business almost ridiculously insignificant. The Malay economic dilemma is still unsolved and seems likely to remain so. The Malays' feeling of frustration continues to deepen.

Malaysia is a democratic country which believes in free enterprise. Free enterprise implies competition in commerce and industry. Free competition in such an economic system determines the price levels of goods, the wages, the distribution of wealth and the opportunities for employment and investment. By and large a free enterprise system is self-sustaining and self-correcting. Still, Government interference is at times required to correct adverse trends and also to ensure that competition is not too destructive or one-sided. Protective tariffs, pioneer status, labour laws and even financial aid by the Government, which may lead even to actual Government participation, are all possible in a free enterprise economy. Actual Government

51

limitation of free enterprise is also possible, but in Malaysia such limitations are not often resorted to as it is generally recognized that the Government is incapable of energizing the maximum economy required in business. Thus the *de facto* nationalization of the railway services, port services and power supplies etc., which constitute limitations on free enterprise, are not favoured even by the Government.

The Malays are as much as everyone else for a free enterprise system. But it is becoming more and more apparent that the competition which should be between individuals and business groups has developed into a competition between racial groups in which one group has an absolute advantage over the other. This can hardly be termed fair competition. Even in America where the free enterprise system has had maximal acceptance, cartels and monopolies by any group or groups are prohibited. In Malaysia however the facts are seldom mentioned for fear of racial conflict. What is forgotten is that failure to face these facts can lead to the very conflict that everyone wants to avoid.

During the British regime there was no real competition between the British firms and the local firms. The British firms were protected, not legally but by race loyalty or chauvinism. The British businessmen and the British administration together ensured that certain businesses remained in British hands. The terms of contract or conditions of these businesses were such as to ensure that the local businessmen were prevented from entering and competing in British preserves. Independence in 1957 put an end to British monopoly, but the Chinese became the principal beneficiaries. In a plural Malaysian society this can hardly be regarded as fair. Every race should have a share in the bounty. The stock answer is that Malaysia believes in free enterprise and its concurrent competition. But is it easier to compete with the Chinese as a community, since it was not easy to compete with the British during the colonial regime? An examination of Chinese methods and principles should serve to indicate the actual situation.

Unlike Western businessmen, the Chinese do not care much for the public limited company with its massive ramifications and its ability to survive the original founder. Chinese business is basically a family enterprise, and as the family is an extremely important unit in Chinese society the foundation of the business is fairly solid, at least during the life-time of the founder. Beyond the family, the Chinese is tied to his clan, his province of origin or dialect group, and finally to his race. All these ties are of extreme importance in the actual conducting of his business. They constitute a diminishing order of exclusiveness. Within his race family loyalty comes first, but the greatest division is between his race and others. The Chinese will not suffer the presence of anyone not of his own race in his business unless it is absolutely unavoidable.

Besides these family and ethnic ties, Chinese businesses are controlled by a number of guilds and chambers of commerce. The guilds are an important cog in the Chinese business wheel. They are designed to minimize competition in a particular trade, and to lessen the cost of overheads by the provision of certain facilities paid for in subscriptions from the members. In any particular trade a percentage of the value of merchandize handled by a member goes to the guild. Part of the money collected goes towards the running of cheap lodging houses for members and their employees travelling on business. The guilds can prevent a non-member retailer from getting the products he wishes to retail. As the retailing outlets are almost exclusively Chinese and the guild is a racial organization, the effect is to exclude all other races from entering certain specialized trades.

The proliferation of all types of business in Malaya, especially after Independence, means that it is almost impossible to establish and run guilds for the newer trades. The problem is overcome by the Chinese through a strong interconnected system of chambers of commerce which are not, however, solely devoted to promoting and protecting Chinese business. Time and again they have taken the role of, and have been accepted as the spokesman for, the Chinese community on matters other than business. Their racialist role often exceeds their commercial role. They have branched off into politics, and they have stood up for Chinese culture and language. It is to be expected that these organizations should also promote and sustain extreme racial exclusiveness in business. Covert Chinese chauvinism is in fact their *raison d'etre*. The stress is more on Chinese than on commerce. This being so, they supplement the already almost water-tight racialist set-up of the Chinese family businesses and the guilds. Between these three, the chambers of commerce, the guilds and family loyalty, the exclusion of non-Chinese from almost all Chinese-run business becomes complete.

Chinese business relies heavily on secret deals and private arrangements. In this, the fact that their businesses are mainly family concerns is of extreme importance. Family loyalty ensures that the deals, however unethical, are not divulged to others to the detriment of the business. Even in the retail business, the employment of only members of the family permits flexibility in the pricing of goods which renders any organized undercutting difficult. The system of accounting is crude but effective. The flexible prices also permit expenditure which could otherwise not be accounted for to be included in the prices of goods. In fact the accounting, especially in a family retail business, is almost meaningless to outsiders. Its main importance is that it fulfills Government requirements, and it indicates roughly the types and amount of stock which have passed through the shop. In any case, in most instances a different set of books are kept for Government inspection.

In business, being established is all-important. The Chinese are established, and have so penetrated all the retail business and most of the wholesale business, that they can dictate terms in the marketing of anything. It behoves everyone with anything to sell to deal with the Chinese. To deal with anyone else is not only to diminish outlets but to limit customers too, for the Chinese, because of their wealth, are naturally the biggest ultimate consumers. As the Chinese naturally prefer Chinese shops,

54

those who fail to get Chinese shops to retail their goods will not succeed in making good profits.

Petrol distribution is one example. Because of Government encouragement, a number of petrol service stations are run by Malays. The Chinese do not completely boycott these stations, but these stations cannot hope to win contracts to supply the fleets of lorries and buses belonging to Chinese transport companies. The sale of oil to these companies is usually the source of maintenance income for the service stations. The non-Chinese stations cannot therefore do as well as the Chinese service stations. The business connections are just not there. It is the same with all other businesses. The means to boycott are partially or entirely in the hands of the Chinese, and they have never hesitated to use them. Except when absolutely necessary the Chinese will not do business with non-Chinese. Even European firms find it easier to employ Chinese executives in order to facilitate dealing with Chinese wholesalers and distributors.

It is necessary to say a few words about Chinese retail business in order to complete this short study of Chinese business methods. The Chinese retail shop is invariably a family affair. As such, wages are unknown. The proprietor and all the members of his family work for the food that is provided and no more. The saving is tremendous and the amount of goods sold, and the size of the shop as well as operational capital increase very rapidly. There is no fixed price for anything, and most certainly the prices are not marked on the goods. This permits flexibility in price, but family loyalty ensures that any excess profit does not go to the salesman. The weights and measures used are easily manipulated so that even if something is apparently sold below cost, the shop will not really lose.

Credit facilities are encouraged as a means of ensuring continued custom. A non-Chinese shop or a cooperative shop finds this impossible to compete with. In the village this credit soon develops into a form of barter in which payment is made by selling whatever yearly crop is harvested. From credit in supplies the retailer graduates to cash credit, and in no time at all the little village shop-keeper becomes the purchasing agent, money-lender and indirect landlord of the village. No business can go on in the village without his being involved in it. Indeed in many instances the titles to all the farm lands near his shop are kept with him as collateral even though it is not legal for him to do so. Once this happens, it is useless for anyone other than another Chinese to try and compete against him in the retail business. He is now permanently established and immovable. His own customers and debtors will cry out in anguish if he is removed.

Chinese business methods and the extent of their control of the economy of the country is such that competition between their community and other communities is quite impossible. Their close-knit communal business tie-ups and connections, their extensive hold over the wholesale and retail business, their control of transportation, their powerful banks and their own wealth are such as to con-stitute an impregnable barrier against any substantial encroachment by other communities in their economic preserves in a free enterprise society. In fact free enter-prise in Malaysia is only confined to the Chinese community. For the other communities the economy of the country follows a system of monopoly in enterprise which is not tolerated even in America. In fact Chinese monopoly is even greater than the monopoly practised by the British during the colonial period. The British confined themselves to big business and left retail trade to the Chinese. With the Chinese, every form of business from hawking fruits to multi-million dollar construction work is monopolized by them. Not even the crumbs are left to others.

The Malay attitude to this situation varies from compla-cency and acceptance of their exclusion from commerce and industry, to deep resentment and envy of Chinese economic hegemony. Complacency is less common now because Government jobs on which the Malays rely are getting more scarce for a variety of reasons. As more and more Malays face unemployment, the attitude towards Ma-lay exclusion in business seems to harden. But as usual,

politeness and a genuine desire to be accommodating have
prevented the Malays from openly voicing their thoughts.
And this unwillingness to be unpleasant is most evident
among people best able to effect changes for the betterment
of the Malays. More often than not the intellectuals and the
political leaders are on the defensive, apologizing even for
picking up the crumbs that have been thrown to the Malays.

Year after year, as statistics show increases in the
living standards in Malaysia, no one dares to demand that
figures be published on a racial basis. Everyone knows
that these average increases are misleading. The per capita income, for example, changes rapidly as a few people
become millionaires while the rest remain poor. In the
same way the rapid increase of income of one community
is made to appear as a moderate increase in the income of
all communities. In fact, a slight increase in the GNP or
per capita income can mean a much greater disparity in
the average product and income of each community.

It is wrong to imagine that the Malays do not know that
these figures are misleading. If they do not point this out
it is because, as has been stated before, they abhor unpleasantness. Together with this dislike for facing up to
the hard facts of life, there is their traditional apathy. So
far we have spoken of the difficulties and impediments which
have been placed in their way. It would not be entirely fair
to blame only others for Malay economic backwardness.
The Malays must admit to a fair share in this blame. From
the leaders to the ordinary *kampong* dwellers, Malays
have displayed an attitude that augments even the slightest
efforts of others to displace them in the economic field.

Malays are ever ready to use new products and the new
skills of others but not to learn to acquire new skills themselves. We know from available evidence that Malays were
skilled goldsmiths, but as soon as the Chinese goldsmiths
came, the relatively better products of the Chinese soon
displaced the Malay products. No attempt was made to
learn from the Chinese. It is true that the Chinese have
never been willing teachers of any skill they have, but
when they were few in number, it would have been a simple

57

matter to make them divulge their techniques. Instead, as the Chinese with their better workmanship took away the customers of the Malays, the Malays were content to pack up and go out of business. In time it became impossible to find any Malay jeweller wherever there were Chinese. Over and over again this happened with every type of work. When houses were made of wood there were Malay carpenters capable of truly fine work involving the most intricate carving and joinery. But when brick and mortar came into fashion Malays did not learn to use these materials. Today, when materials for construction are so varied and complex the Malays find that even if they wish to, they can no longer build anything on their own. At one stage or another they will need Chinese craftsmen. The Chinese have become indispensable not only to the nation but to the Malays themselves.

The rapid advances in mechanization and electronics have made matters even worse. The electric fan is a common feature in Malay houses. They have learnt to switch it on and off, but know nothing about repairing or making it. At the same time, the few Malays who used to make fans out of palm leaves have stopped doing so because no one needs their products any more. This process is repeated with every new modern amenity or implement which is introduced. The desire to keep up is not there. An extreme lassitude has descended on the Malays which seems to indicate that they are just not good enough for anything.

But is this really so? Are they not good enough for anything? There is a reverse side to this phenomenon. Malays, except for those in Kelantan, may not be able to actually build a brick house on their own, but Malay architects are planning and directing the whole complex operation. Malay engineers can plan and direct the building of bridges of the most modern design. Malay agriculturists can conduct experiments and direct the cultivation of any and every crop. Malay doctors and lawyers compare well with those of any race. Malay administrators are much better than others. The potential is there but only in a limited field is it developed. Between the traditional Malay agriculturists and the

58

educated *elite* there is a vast lacuna in which Malays are not to be found. Their potential in this area has not been developed. It is due partly to their apathy, and partly to the short-sightedness and apathy of their leaders. The fact is that even their responsible leaders suffer from the same lassitude that permeates their community.

Malay leaders have been known to say that Malays are not suited for business or skilled work. They are agriculturists. Money does not mean the same thing to them as it does to the Chinese. They do not have the wish or the capacity for hard work. And above all they cannot change.

But again is this true? Politics have shown that the Malays can change. It is difficult to imagine a race more disinterested in politics than the Malays were before the war. They saw the country with a detachment that can only be described as phenomenal. They did not seem to care what happened. Instead of feeling resentment against their colonial masters, they were actually full of praise for the British. They even felt proud to be a part of the British Empire. Roff in his book *The Origins of Malay Nationalism* clearly describes how the Malay masses generally considered politics as being none of their concern, and the pains any Malay took to explain that he was not dabbling in politics at all. They were so accommodating that the British took them for granted and did not foresee any opposition, even to their design to deprive the Malays of their own country. But, in the event, the reaction of the Malays was such a complete reversal of accepted ideas about them that there has to be a revision and re-evaluation of these ideas. And a quality that must certainly be re-evaluated is their capacity for change.

The change in Malay political interest has confounded people not only by its vehemence but also by its permanent quality. Long after the original objective had been won the Malays have continued to be politically active and organized. Political parties penetrate the remotest Malay *kampong* where even illiterate Malays hold meetings, elect office-bearers bearing exotic titles, and form branches which function as essential cogs in the vast national political machinery. They are even capable of forgetting their primary loyalty to their states in a much bigger loyalty to a newly-created nation of which most of them at one time were hardly aware. Elections, unthinkable just over a decade ago, were not only readily accepted, but were also actually carried out and participated in with gusto by every Malay. In short, the change in the Malays' attitude to politics is radical and complete.

The question is whether they can change equally well in other fields. To this the only answer is: Why not? In the field of commerce and industry what is needed is a general awareness of their economic plight by the Malays and their leaders, and of the disaster that must befall them and the nation if they remain complacent. If the leaders are to turn their attention to leading the Malays to a better life it will need but little effort to study the causes and prescribe the remedies. The measures must be drastic, as were the measures taken by the Malay leaders during the political crisis involving the Malayan Union. The truth must be told and told in no uncertain terms. The Malays must be aware of their own faults as much as the faults of others. Where necessary, laws must be promulgated in order to render effective whatever economic policy may be considered necessary. Harsh punitive measures should be meted out to those who impede the elevation of the Malays to an equality with the other races. Given sensible leaders with a comprehensive understanding of the problems and the will to tackle them, there should be no disruption of the steady economic growth of the country. Indeed, as the Malays are pulled up to the level of other Malaysians, the effect should be to boost and render more accurate, the favourable statistics of national income and production that each year embellish budget speeches.

But the dilemma of the Malays is that not only is there little effort made to right the economic wrongs from which they suffer, but it is also wrong to even mention that economic wrongs exist at all. The whole idea seems to be that the less they talk about it the more the country will benefit from the economic stability built on Chinese economic domination. What is important, the Malays are told, is that Malaysia must prosper as a nation, and amateurs like them in business are not likely to contribute to this prosperity. All these arguments are completely true. If no impediment at all is placed in the way of total Chinese domination of the economy of Malaysia, the country would certainly be prosperous. The Malay dilemma is whether they should stop trying to help themselves in order that they should be proud to be the poor citizens of a prosperous country or whether they should try to get at some of the riches that this country boasts of, even if it blurs the economic picture of Malaysia a little. For the Malays it would appear there is not just an economic dilemma, but a Malay dilemma.

5: The Meaning of Racial Equality

Racial equality is a prerequisite of racial harmony, of national unity. No one really disputes this. The harmony between master and servant, between rich and poor, between rulers and ruled is not true harmony. It is merely acceptance of the unalterable, so long as it seems unalterable. Sooner or later changing values and ideas result in the rejection of the *status quo* and a move is made towards a more equitable situation. As equality must mean a gain for the have-nots and a loss for the haves, the process of achieving it produces a strain in the previously "harmonious" relationship. Once equality is achieved society is less subjected to stresses and strains and harmony is more likely to be the result. There will still be conflict but at least one recognized cause of it will have been removed.

Unfortunately, although racial equality is recognized as indispensable to racial harmony, there is still little understanding of what is meant by racial equality. Each community or individual interprets racial equality to the advantage of the interpreter. Thus on the question of scholarships for example, racial equality for some means the equality to compete for the scholarships regardless of race. Now if this interpretation is accepted, the end result in Malaysia at least, will not be racial equality but actually an aggravation of racial disparity. In other words equality in one field may result in greater disparity in another.

Racial disparity is not characteristic of Malaysia alone. It is to be found in most countries where different races live together. The fact that it is so common means that there is no easy solution. Besides, no two countries have similar causes of racial conflict. Nevertheless a study of the situation in other countries should be profitable, if not in solving our problems, at least in a wider understanding of what constitutes the problem.

In the following pages I have made an attempt to define

the meaning of racial equality largely by reference to the racial problem in the United States of America. It is not unbiased, but as so much has been said about the Malays being a privileged people in Malaysia, it is perhaps time to hear the Malay view of these privileges and of racial equality. It is then up to the earnest and the honest to appraise them, and then formulate a solution to the problem.

In any nation with more than one ethnic-cultural group the question of racial equality constitutes an issue of vital importance. Since the birth of Malaysia, indeed even before Malaya became independent, this question has been a continuous focus of much bitterness and political wrangling. Twelve years of independence and comparative racial harmony have not diminished the political controversy this question provokes. The events of 13 May 1969 brought this problem into the open. Now more than ever, it is time that there should be a clear understanding of the meaning of racial equality in Malaysia.

Racial equality implies certain values, and values differ according to the standards which a given community accepts. To understand the meaning of racial equality it is important to know what the values being compared are. It is also illuminating to compare these values with the values of other countries.

The United States is the first country which comes to mind when one talks of racial equality. In the United States all citizens, irrespective of colour, race or religion are equal before the law. There are of course a few states where even the law is discriminatory, but the Federal Constitution as interpreted by the court accords the Negroes equal status with every other American citizen. The racial inequality in the United States is not one resulting from discriminatory laws but from social and economic ostracism. If the violence of the reaction is any indication, social and economic segregation are equally or even more hateful than inequality before the law.

What is the position of the Negroes in the United States? As has already been pointed out, the American Constitution with its Thirteenth, Fourteenth and Fifteenth Amendments

63

gives the Negroes equal status with all other citizens of the United States. The earlier interpretation of the Constitution was biased, but the Federal Courts have got over the prejudices which affected earlier judges. The present interpretation leaves no doubt that all citizens irrespective of colour, race, creed or origin are equal before the law and have equal rights as citizens. The Bill of Rights embodied in the Fourteenth Amendment further clarifies the rights of citizens. As the Constitution is the supreme law of the United States, and as the Supreme Court has jurisdiction over all the states of the union, discriminatory laws and practices in individual states can be and have been nullified by resort to the Federal Constitution. In other words, there can be no doubt that, legally, racial equality prevails in the United States. If there are agitations and riots because of racial inequality in the United States, it is not because the Constitution is discriminatory, but because there is a conscious discrimination, socially and economically, against Negroes.

Social and economic discrimination are as effective and humiliating as legal discrimination. Indeed they can be even more effective than legal discrimination. The ghettoes were not built as Negro ghettoes. They were quite ordinary residential urban areas open to all citizens. Roxbury in Boston, the Negro quarter of that city, looks like any other urban area in the United States. What makes Roxbury a Negro ghetto is the unspoken decision of the whites to move out of any area into which black people have moved. Thus as soon as the Negroes have enough money to buy their way into the better parts of the city, a white exodus converts the area into a black ghetto. As the buildings vacated will not be occupied by whites, who are richer than the blacks, the value of property depreciates, poor blacks move in, and the Negro urban areas become slums.

What created these ghettoes is nothing more than social ostracism. All over the United States this process went on and is going on. There can be no law to force people to stay in any place they wish to vacate. There can also be no means to force the whites to remain near the Negroes.

Ghettoes will therefore continue to form in the United States and to cause racial inequality despite any laws.

There are other examples of social discrimination in the United States. Economic ostracism is another contributor to racial inequality in the United States, and like social ostracism, it takes many forms. If one tries to elucidate the reasons for this economic discrimination, one is invariably told that it is not racial but purely economic. The Negroes are inferior, unintelligent, lazy, incapable of knowing the value of money, of acquiring skills and of adjusting to new methods and ideas. No one wants to employ them unless it is unavoidable. It is cheaper in the long run to employ whites because their work output is greater and their standards are higher. And as there is no likelihood of there being an absolute shortage of white workers in any field, the need to take in many Negroes is small.

The short answer to this is that if the Negroes are so incapable of work why were they brought to America in the first place? We know that the Negroes were transported from the jungles of darkest Africa to work on the estates and in the houses of the American settlers. They became not only good field workers, but also cooks and housekeepers.

If the Negroes lag in skill and competence today, it is because they have been segregated socially and economically for generations. Generations of whites progressed with the times, changing their mode of living, receiving appropriate education and acquiring new skills as America moved from an agricultural economy to a highly sophisticated industrial economy. As the gap between the capacities of the Negroes and the whites widens, apathy descends on the former, making them less and less inclined to adjust themselves and bridge the gap. And this very apathy and seeming incapacity to learn and adjust are now used to keep the Negroes segregated economically, thus perpetuating and augmenting the difference between them and the whites.

Inevitably a few Negroes achieved a breakthrough, and it is they who most see and feel the resentment of their community, and desire to right the wrongs which have been wrought on Negroes through the generations. And equally inevitably they resorted to political action with a degree of violence that startled the world. Riots, arson and even murder are not excluded as means of fighting for racial equality.

The obvious conclusion is that legal equality is not enough. To be equal means to have a share in everything, in the good things of life as well as the responsibilities. A fair share in the good things of life must not only be the intention of the Government, but it must also be the intention of the people as a whole. And that intention must always be visibly interpreted. The Government and the people of America vow before the world that they have no intention of treating the Negroes as inferior citizens. If the Negroes do not have their share of the prosperity of the country it is their own fault. But this placing of the entire blame on the Negroes is neither correct nor acceptable. It is the institution of economic and social ostracism that has been, through the generations, the unbridgeable gap between the Negroes and the whites. And that gap is self-widening, making a solution to the problem more and more difficult to achieve as time passes by. It is not enough just to say "we have no objections, come and get it, it's all yours if you are prepared to do as we do". We know very well that the Negroes cannot cross the gulf of generations of economic, social and educational backwardness merely by saying "I will".

The American Government apparently realizes its responsibility to help the Negroes bridge the gap. Millions of dollars have been voted, and a host of new projects and schemes have been initiated to give the Negroes the type of training necessary to fit them into the spectrum of American economic prosperity. But all these Government efforts will come to nothing unless the American people as a whole cease to discriminate against the Negroes. Shops, factories, offices and hotels must accept Negroes for every level of work. More important still, some sort of allowance must be made for the Negroes during the early period of adjustment. In fact what is needed is not merely equal treatment but actually a considerable bending over backwards in order to accommodate the Negroes. As discrimination has taken generations to widen the gap between the Negroes and the whites, so the process of conscious accommodation must take several generations before the effects will show. Once this has happened, true racial equality will have been established.

Legal equality is meaningless in the face of social and economic ostracism practised by racial groups under conditions which are not within the range of the law. An employer who refuses to take in a Negro can always come up with a whole string of apparently valid reasons. If the Government and society are willing to accept these reasons at face value, then racial inequality will persist, leading to discontent, resentment, riots, arson and death. An enlightened Government and society must insist on positive steps to integrate; indeed both should act to eliminate inequality in order to over-correct as a means of countering inevitable repercussions in the future. In effect this means that the Government and society must scrutinize not merely public action but also private action so as to ensure that racial equality prevails. A shop proprietor who employs a single assistant should be as much under suspicion of racial discrimination as the huge industrial complexes employing thousands of workers. Liberal opinion in America is indeed moving in this direction, but the number of liberal Americans is not enough for effects to be felt throughout the nation.

There is another area of racial inequality in the United States which seldom receives publicity. The Red Indians suffer as much from racial inequality as the Negroes, but being fewer in number and confined to areas off the beaten track of newspapermen, their degradation has not been brought to light. The strange thing about the Red Indians is that they are in fact a privileged people in the United States. They own land denied to others, and they are even exempted from certain taxes. Legally then they are more "equal" than other citizens of the United States. Nevertheless, far from being a super-race in America, they are in fact pariahs. A typical opinion of white Americans when asked about the Indian is that they (the Indians) are beyond redemption, and that if you give them money they would rather buy a Cadillac than improve themselves.

However, if a white man wins a lottery he will not necessarily immediately go into business in order to consolidate his gain. He will most probably use up most of his winnings on the luxuries which he had previously coveted. The Indian reaction is not peculiarly Indian. It is human. What seems to be lacking is a desire to help the Indian integrate with the rest of American society. In other words, Indians, despite enjoying a privileged status, are regarded as inferior, and unworthy of being equal partners within American society.

If the Red Indians have not reacted as violently as the Negroes, it is because their numbers are small, and because they are scattered and widely separated geographically as well as tribally. The visitor to America can stay there for months without meeting a single Indian. But nevertheless their resentment is real. Buffy St Marie, a Red Indian folk singer well-known throughout the United States, sings of the land which has been taken from her forefathers and wonders what the Indians have got in return. Racial inequality obviously hurts the Red Indians as much as it does the Negroes. It is not enough to be legally privileged, it is also necessary for equality to be real. It is clearly necessary for the Indians to have their fair share of the economic prosperity which characterizes the America of the whites. The privilege that the Indians have should not be used to preserve them as historical pieces which add colour to the American scene. They should be truly integrated into American society, economically, socially and politically.

So what is racial equality? Is it a legal quantity that can be defined, categorized and defended by law? If it is, the Red Indians would be the super-race of America. But we know from the violence of Negro agitation as much as from the muted cry of the Indians, that legal status is not enough. To be equal is to be accepted into every strata of society socially, economically and politically to a degree which more or less reflects the proportion of the population made up by the various groups. It is not enough that the American Armed Forces should have Negro officers leading white soldiers. It is not enough for the American President to have Negro bureau heads and presidential aides. It is not enough to have Negro judges and ambassadors. It is also necessary to have Negro executives in private industries, Negro airline pilots and hostesses, Negro shopkeepers and restaurant operators, Negro engineers, lawyers and doctors. It is necessary too that all these categories of people should not be segregated in their places of employment or live in ghettoes or reserves.

In America today this is what white and black liberals think, and this is also what the American Government professes. But the average white American is still bent on discrimination, on being exclusive and superior. If the Government refuses to legalize the superior status of the whites, it does not really matter. The whites can always privately, individually and collectively, keep the Negroes suppressed. The whites can deny them jobs and the acquisition of skills, deny them business opportunities, deny them credit and know-how, and deny them access to the complex machinery of a modern economy.

How relevant to Malaysia is the racial inequality in the United States? The answer is, "very relevant indeed", for racial inequality anywhere breeds the same things — greater inequality, bitterness and violence. In Malaysia the degree of inequality is not as great as in the United States, but the seeds of violence are nevertheless there.

In Malaysia there can be no denying that the status of the Malays differs from that of the non-Malays. The Malays and the Red Indians of America are more or less in the same category. Malays are accepted as the indigenous people of the country, but the country is no longer exclusively theirs. However, in order to protect and preserve their status, certain laws are necessary.

The most significant of these laws is concerned with Malay Land Reserve. Those acquainted with the history of the Red Indians will see here not only a similarity of terms, but also of historical content. The reason for the original law was not some sort of national privilege accorded to the Malays during the British Colonial period. Immigrants have always been legally entitled to own land. Even after the law came into effect, immigrants and foreigners were still able to obtain titles to land. The law was therefore not a manifestation of national consciousness as are such laws in other countries where only citizens may own land. The Malay Land Reserve Laws were by intention a measure to counter what was becoming quite obvious during the colonial era: that the Malays were losing all their land to richer immigrants and foreigners. Clearly, unless legal measures were adopted, the ultimate result would be that the Malays would become tenants of foreign and immigrant landlords in their own country. In other words, although the Malays called Malaya *Tanah Malayu* or Malay Land, there would in fact be no real land belonging to them. The possibility was distinct and credible at one time.

The original law was not aimed at re-acquiring land which the Malays had lost. It was not even aimed at completely arresting the process of foreign acquisition of land. It was merely intended to ensure that the Malays had some space in which to live and which they could call their own. What was already in the hands of non-Malays, who in those days were also non-citizens, was to remain their property. In addition, provisions were made for the excision of Malay reserves so that the non-citizens would not be completely barred from acquiring new holdings which, in the eyes of the Colonial Government, was considered essential for one reason or another. And the reasons for excision were legion.

The most glaring instance of unfair excision of Malay Reserve land was that involving tin-bearing land in Perak. Whenever tin was found in Malay Reserve land the State Council invariably consented to excise the appropriate portion to enable the British and other non-Malays to acquire the land. In return, an equal acreage of state land was redesignated as Malay Reserve. This new land was selected from areas which were primary jungle, inaccessible and not suspected of having valuable mineral deposits. In other words, valuable Malay Reserve lands were exchanged for worthless jungle of no immediate use to the Malays or anyone else.

In the urban areas, excision of Malay Reserves was a regular feature of the colonial era. Any reason seemed good enough. The most frequent cause was Malay poverty. Malay land owners in the urban areas, attempting to maintain living standards comparable with other urban dwellers, soon got themselves into debt with non-Malay moneylenders. The usual security was the land they held. When debts were not paid, the courts would order that the land be sold by auction. If no Malay could bid sufficiently high, and this was the rule rather than the exception, then the land would be sold to non-Malays who would be entitled to have it excised from Malay reservation. This process occurred not only in the urban areas but also in the rural areas. In Kedah thousands of *relongs* of padi land have passed out of Malay hands because of this provision.

A peculiarity about this type of excision is that if a Malay buys back land excised from Malay Reserves, then the land automatically reverts to its former status. This provision obstructs Malays from re-acquiring excised land. The value of land outside Malay Reserves is normally higher because it is held by a richer and more astute community. This land normally gives a good income to the non-Malay owner. If the land is bought back by the Malays and reverts to Malay Reserve status then its value depreciates. In other words, it never pays for Malays to buy former Malay Reserve land. Once excised, this land in fact becomes non-Malay Reserves.

Does the provision for reservation of land for the Malays make them citizens of a higher class than non-Malays? Does this provision cause racial inequality? It needs no great analysis to conclude that it was racial inequality in the first instance which prompted the enactment of the law. Early in the British Colonial period it became clear that the Malays were going to become landless if left to the mercy of predatory immigrants and the British exploiters. This trend was most obvious in urban areas. In Kuala

Lumpur for example, by 1890 the Malays had almost no land to call their own. At the rate at which the non-Malays were buying up land and Kuala Lumpur was expanding, the Malays were on the way to becoming total strangers to the city which was the State, and later the Federated Malay States, capital. The Government then rapidly created the Malay Reserve of Kampong Bahru.

Elsewhere, the Malay Land Reserve Laws formed a legal basis for keeping some land in Malay hands. As has already been mentioned, ways and means were also provided to get round this law. These ways and means, as well as the wealth of the non-Malays, effectively nullified the superior position which this law at first seemed to give the Malays. The law did not completely prevent the richest land from being excised and transferred to non-Malays. Over the years the effect of this law was to push the Malays into less valuable land while non-Malays, and especially the Europeans, took over tin-bearing land and land easily accessible for rubber plantation. In certain states, despite the Malay Land Reserve Law, there is more land belonging to non-Malays than to Malays. And certainly in terms of actual assessed value there are probably only one or two states where total Malay holdings are greater in value than non-Malay holdings.

Land in the urban areas is always more costly than rural land. The Malay Land Reserve Laws operate in such a way that urban land is readily acquired by non-Malays. Once a non-Malay succeeds in excising land, the value shoots up beyond the range of the poor Malays. Land in urban areas, though small in terms of actual area, is more valuable than the huge tracts of Malay Reserve land in the rural areas.

We can conclude that in the event of an actual evaluation, non-Malays, holding as they do costly urban land and richest producing land, will be found to be in a more privileged position. In other words, despite the existence of the Malay Land Reserve Laws, the Malays are second-class land owners. What is worse is that there is no likelihood that the present laws can correct this position.

The Malay Land Reserve Laws therefore cannot be said to contribute to racial inequality. They were in fact an attempt to correct racial inequality in the first place. In this they have been only partially successful. The misapplication of the law in the past, and the extreme difference in economic wealth between Malay and non-Malay communities, have together blunted the effect of this law. Racial inequality continues despite the law, but it is an inequality that can only be aggravated by removing the laws. The unfortunate position of the Malays, which prompted the laws in the first place, has not been completely corrected. And certainly without these laws the Malays will slide back into worse situations and increase existing inequality.

The other "legal" inequalities are concerned with scholarships and jobs in the Civil Service. These inequalities are basically concerned with education. Educationally the Malays are far behind the other communities. One has but to read the annual school certificate results to realize this. The population of Malaya is almost fifty per cent Malay, yet the results show very much less than fifty per cent Malays among the pass lists. Worse still, the number of Malays with Grade I passes is below that of other communities. Clearly, unless special provisions are made, the chances are that the Malays will never go beyond an elementary education, and will never obtain jobs other than those of the lowest grade in this country.

Part of the reason for this poor showing of Malay students is their chronic poverty and their rural background. The deleterious effect of poverty is not fully understood by most people. In the first place, poor parents are usually not only poor but ill-educated and ill-prepared to look after school-going children. Not understanding the value of education, apathetic, and without much faith in the potential of their children, these parents always fail to furnish even the elementary needs of children going to school. If a child is exceptionally brilliant he may be able to overcome these handicaps, but for the average child, the absence of these basic needs must adversely affect his studies.

The poor Malay parents, ignorant and disinterested, do

not give sufficient moral encouragement to their children in school. They do not urge them to study. They either do not or cannot provide space and amenities for study. In the rural areas they do not even have lights for the children to study by, at night. Not being educated themselves, they cannot even understand, much less help in the studies of their children. They are not able to provide the proper food or medical care when the children are sick. And certainly they cannot afford extra aids for education, such as books and tutors for the backward. In fact poor Malay parents would not even bother about formal schooling for their children were it not for the fact that the Government makes education compulsory.

One of the more effective ways in which the Government is helping education is by granting scholarships. Scholarships are awarded to two different categories of students. Firstly there are scholarships for brilliant students. These are actually prizes, and like most prizes, they are not always won by the most needy. They are nice and very gratifying to have, but not having them would not prove an absolute handicap to most winners. The brilliant students who win this type of scholarship are not always from poor families. Indeed the brilliant student from poor families is the exception to the rule for reasons which have already been made clear. In the educational advancement of a community or nation this type of scholarship cannot be said to be indispensable.

The other type of scholarship is given to students with minimum qualifications, who, for financial reasons, are handicapped. For these students these scholarships are absolutely necessary. They are the means of breaking a vicious cycle. Backwardness in a modern society spells poverty. Poverty leads to poor education. Poor education perpetuates more poverty. Somewhere the cycle has to be broken, and a rich country like Malaysia would stand accused of moral irresponsibility if she did not subsidize the education of the poor. The scholarships which poor Malay children are receiving are morally justifiable and socially necessary. They are the means to progress for a backward community in a progressing nation. They are a means of rectifying racial inequality, and of raising the Malays to the level of the Chinese and Indians.

The question asked is why should the proportion of scholarships given, be so much in favour of the Malays? Is not this proportion a manifestation of racial favouritism and inequality? Are there not also poor Chinese and poor Indians who deserve these scholarships?

To answer these questions one has to go back to the basic reason for the preferential treatment of the Malays. The motive behind preferential treatment is not to put the Malays in a superior position, but to bring them up to the level of the non-Malays. Under the British Colonial regime it had already become obvious that not only were the Malays economically backward, but they were also educationally behind. Although the actual number of Malay students then in school greatly outnumbered non-Malays, these students were only primary vernacular school students. This was because primary vernacular education was free for Malays. This primary education did not help the Malays fit themselves into modern society. Indeed the vast majority of them were not expected to. Except for a very few, the majority were expected to stay in their villages and lead the poverty-stricken life of their forefathers.

On the other hand, the non-Malays being economically well-off, profited more from the secondary education introduced by the British. Indeed, they went on to achieve as high an education as their wealth permitted. True, not all the non-Malays were wealthy and able to acquire a good education. But, because a good number were, the educational standard of the Malays began to fall far behind that of the non-Malays. It goes without saying that if the small number of non-Malays who are financially handicapped are assisted towards achieving what their richer countrymen have achieved, then the disparity between the educational status of the Malays and the non-Malays would increase even more.

It is therefore not for reasons of Malay superiority that preferential treatment for Malays in scholarship awards was insisted upon. The scholarships are not a manifestation of racial inequality. They are a means of breaking down the superior position of the non-Malays in the field of education. The Malays are not proud of this treatment. They are not proud of the "privilege" of being protected by law like cripples. They would like to get rid of these privileges if they can, but they have to let pride take second place to the facts of life.

If the disproportionate award of scholarships is not sufficient evidence of a type of racial inequality, then what about the Malaysian Civil Service? Here the provision is such that Malays occupy four places in the civil service to every one occupied by a non-Malay. Surely this means putting the administration of the country firmly in the hands of people who form less than half the total population.

If preference on a racial basis is abominable, jobs should go to the people who are best qualified. The important thing is that a job should be well done. But then of course everyone would admit that there are certain extenuating circumstances when this should not apply. Let us examine the principle behind these extenuating circumstances.

Before Independence the British ruled this country well. They may not have given the non-British inhabitants the best of everything, but certainly they were expert administrators. They got jobs done efficiently. They built up an efficient civil service and a completely effective law-enforcing body. They brought law and order to the strife-torn tin-mining areas of Perak and Selangor, settled the minor wars of Malay rajas, and put down piracy. They built roads and railways and collected taxes which actually reached the treasury and were spent on public services. They were certainly a people well suited to administer.

But we were not satisfied just because jobs were well done by the people best able to do them. We had our pride to think of. We wanted to rule this country ourselves. We might not do it as efficiently but that was irrelevant. What was important was not merely the achievement of Independence. We wanted Malayanization as well. And we wanted it rapidly, according to a fixed time-table. The implication is

76

that we did not care whether we could do the job equally well, we merely wanted to take over because we were Malayans. In other words, under these circumstances we should discriminate in favour of ourselves. We blatantly declared that there should be job preference on a basis of race. It was racial prejudice which formed the basis of Malayanization.

The prejudice would have stopped there had there been just one community in this country, or if the different communities were equally well able to take advantage of Malayanization without causing an imbalance in the distribution of the jobs vacated by the British. Unfortunately, it was all too clear that because of the difference in economic wealth which had in turn affected the education of the different communities, the jobs falling vacant with Malayanization could be properly filled by just one community. This would be alright if there was an affinity between all the communities as Malayans. But the fact is, the Malays were more remote from the Chinese than they were from the British.

More Malays could speak English than could speak Chinese. Malays had worked with and under the British in the Government, but this had never happened in Chinese establishments. To the Malays and to the nation as a whole, to exchange a British administration for a Chinese administration after Malayanization would have been simply ridiculous. Independence would be meaningless to the Malays if they were to be ruled by Chinese Malayans who were even more remote from them, and whose interests more often clashed with theirs than British interests had done. Independence would only be worthwhile if the Malays had a share in the running of the Government. Provision therefore had to be made to ensure that jobs were distributed not merely on a basis of ability but also on that of race.

Even though the Malays wanted a racial bias in the distribution of jobs formerly held by the British, they did not totally disregard qualifications. They only insisted on this procedure in fields where they could reasonably do a good job. The purely administrative service is one such field.

In order that they would not be left too far behind because they were unprepared to enter other fields, the quota they asked for in the administrative service was high. Yet despite this high quota of four Malays to one non-Malay, the number of Malays in the Government (Civil) Service is low compared to the percentage of Malays in this country.

In Malaya the Malay community forms about forty-eight per cent of the population while the Chinese make up only thirty-eight per cent. But in Divisions I and II of the Government Service, the divisions most concerned with the direction and execution of Government policy, the Malays make up only one-third the total number of officers and draw one-third of the salary paid out. By no stretch of the imagination could it be said that the quota of Malays in the Civil (Administration) Service contributes to or constitutes racial inequality. It is obviously a device to correct existing and potential racial inequality. One look at the annual school certificate results of the students in higher educational institutions should be enough to give a picture of the Malaysian Government Service without the Civil Service quota. It is possible, with racial prejudice as evident as it is now, that without the quota provisions there would be no Malays in Government Service at all. This would certainly be the ultimate in racial inequality. To the Malays, Malayanization would be a mockery because the Government would still be as foreign as the British Government once was. Worse, even the paternalism of the British would be gone.

Besides the Malay Land Reserve Laws, and the quota system for scholarships and the Civil Service, there are other laws which might appear to discriminate in favour of the Malays. Yet discriminatory laws and policies in Malaya are not meant to give advantage to one community over another. They are designed in fact to prevent this happening. They have, to a certain degree, been able to correct many unfair advantages but they have certainly not succeeded completely. It is clear to anyone living in, or even visiting Malaya that there is no racial equality in this country, just as in the United States, despite non-discriminatory laws, there is as yet no racial equality.

Laws do not make people equal. They can only make equality possible. In the final analysis it is the people, and the people alone who make themselves equal.

Racial equality can only be said to exist when each race not only stands equal before the law, but also when each race is represented in every strata of society, in every field of work, in proportion more or less to their percentage of the population. If this interpretation of racial equality is correct, then what is it in Malaya that makes racial inequality so obvious? Before discussing specific fields it is relevant to consider the general picture first. The striking thing about the general picture is the geographical distribution of the races. The towns are non-Malay, but the rural areas are almost completely Malay. This demographic peculiarity is in itself evidence of racial inequality.

In this modern age it does not take long to discern that the most progressive nations are those with maximum urbanization. The United States of America started off with ninety-five per cent of its population involved in agriculture in the rural areas. Today only five per cent of its population is truly rural. The strength of the United States is in the cities, where commerce and industry form the backdrop to everything that is of significance to the national and international life of the Americans. Even Soviet Russia, essentially an agrarian country when the Soviet Revolution started, is now highly urbanized. Europe of course has been an example of urban strength for much longer than other parts of the world.

The fact that in Malaya the Malays are mainly rural and the non-Malays are urban, means that there is an inequality in the progress and development of the communities. A developing nation or community should have gradually urbanized itself. But despite the fact of being under the same political system during the British regime, the Malays have not followed the course of development which characterized other rural agrarian communities in other parts of the world.

The importance of urbanization in the progress of a

community lies in the more complex organization which the towns and cities provide. This makes urban dwellers sharper and more knowledgeable. The rural dwellers on the other hand are cut off from these experiences and are subjected only to the age-old pattern of life that characterizes the country-side. Their sum total of knowledge is therefore minimal and their capacity for change limited. The rural community is thus more static when compared with the urban community. In short, there is inequality of development between the urban and the rural areas.

Racial inequality is here an inequality of wealth, an inequality of opportunities, and an inequality of development. The significance of demographic distribution in the search for the true reason for racial inequality is very great indeed. It is as much a cause as it is a result of racial inequality. It can be said with some justification that if the distribution of the population of Malaya is in itself evidence of racial inequality, then the Malays are to blame for it. It seems obvious at first glance that they chose freely to remain in, or even move into the rural areas. They have thus brought racial inequality upon themselves by being rural and retarding their own progress. While the other communities have developed with the progress characteristic of cities and towns, the Malays have, it seems, been content to just watch this progress. Nothing appears to prevent them from participating by migrating into the urban areas, but they have not done so.

Are these assumptions entirely correct? It is normal for people to be attracted to the bright lights of the towns and the cities, but are the Malays the exception to the rule? Do they really want to remain in the rural areas and to remain backward? To answer these questions, one has to look into the alternatives which face the Malay community in the choice of habitat.

Firstly there are the Malay Land Reserve Laws. These laws have prevented the Malays from losing all their land and becoming complete tenants to non-Malay landlords. But the laws have not worked entirely in favour of the Malays. We have seen how the laws can convert unreserved land into non-Malay Reserve. As Government policy tends to create these non-Malay Reserves in the urban areas, the Malays, even if they are rich enough, prefer to settle on the land reserved for them in the rural areas; land which is cheap and readily available. Even if they already have land in the urban areas, the availability of cheap land in nearby rural areas tempts them into selling their urban holdings and moving out of the towns. Their land in the towns would fetch a considerable price when sold to non-Malays. If they show a tendency to cling to their urban holdings, the price would be raised until the temptation to sell becomes too great. Even if their urban holdings are within the Malay Reserve they would still be asked to sell. They would be shown ways of getting round the law with considerable profit until their resolve breaks. The Malay Land Reserve Laws are quite ineffective in keeping the Malays in the urban areas. Only rigid laws such as govern the Malay Reserve in Kampong Bahru in Kuala Lumpur can succeed in keeping the Malays within urban areas.

Apart from the Malay Land Reserve Laws there are of course other factors which force the Malays to move out of urban areas. The lack of jobs is one. Urban society is highly organized and specialized. Everyone has a job which is useful to someone else. It might be a purely service job such as driving a car, lorry or trishaw, or being a menial servant. It could be preparation and sale of food or goods. It might be entertaining or managing entertainment facilities. It might be anything so long as the end result is the earning of money which will buy food and shelter. The situation is entirely different in the rural areas. Food and shelter may be obtained almost for nothing. A small plot of land and a little attap hut is all that is needed to keep body and soul together.

What are the opportunities for jobs for the Malays in the urban areas? The best chances for the Malays are in Government Service where they are not discriminated against and the jobs are comparatively well paid and secure. Outside Government service the only jobs open to them are of the lowest type. They may work as drivers or trishaw peddlers. There may be a few openings in the big European firms. Beyond these, there is no place for the Malays to work and earn a living in the towns and cities. The innumerable Chinese and Indian shops refuse to employ Malays. Until recently the Indians used to import their employees from India. The Chinese will not employ Malay shop assistants for a variety of reasons. The most frequent reason is that Malays do not know how to sell things. But the Malays are also excluded from the jobs which need no skill in salesmanship. Modernized Chinese firms and banks will not employ Malays even as clerks, much less as executives. As the commercial activities in Malayan towns are almost entirely in non-Malay hands, this discrimination means that thousands of jobs are closed to the Malays. As jobs are necessary for urban living, the result of this discrimination is to push the few Malays in the towns to the rural areas and to prevent the influx of rural people into urban areas.

Perhaps the Malays, in order to live in the towns, should go into business, should start shops of their own and so provide opportunities of employment for Malays. If it is accepted that there should be no integration between races, and that in business they should stay in watertight compartments, then Malay shops in urban areas might be just the thing. Unfortunately the starting of business enterprises however small is anything but simple. For the Malays, their position of inferiority in the field of trade and industry make such ventures even more hazardous. They would not only have to compete with people who have larger capital, but also with business traditions and experience second to none in this country. The Chinese are the people to do business with. They have a multiplicity of interlocking organizations which look after interests which are extremely communal. There are guilds and associations in almost every trade and there are powerful Chambers of Commerce. The wholesale trade is entirely in their hands, and the lack of fixed prices as well as the flexibility of their credit system mean that retailers can easily be manipulated by them.

These, and a variety of other racial traits, put the Malay innocent who has the audacity to compete with the non-

82

Malays, in an extremely disadvantageous position. The chances of surviving in the highly competitive field of trade and commerce in the urban areas are minimal even for the experienced and financially sound non-Malays. For the Malays these chances are reduced to almost nothing. A few may struggle along, but the majority could never even leave the planning stage. If the only way to urbanize the Malays is to have Malay enterprises in the towns and cities, then the chances of a significant success are almost certainly nil. The only way for Malays to live in the urban areas is for the non-Malays not to discriminate against them.

How prevalent is this discrimination against Malays? In business it is so great that it is taken for granted. A Chinese establishment, whether big or small, will just not employ any Malay except perhaps as drivers and no one will even say it is discrimination. Admittedly, the reason is often more practical than racial. Chinese businesses are conducted in Chinese with the accounting and records all in Chinese. Business connections are also almost all Chinese. Besides, the smaller Chinese shops are family concerns which depend a great deal on family loyalty as a basis for honesty.

Nevertheless, it is possible to employ Malays if there is a wish to do so. The ordinary retail shops could easily employ Malay salesmen. They may not be as good as the Chinese, but they will certainly never be any good unless they have opportunities to learn. There will be drop-outs, perhaps a considerable number at the beginning. But it is reasonable to expect a few at least to persist and succeed. In the bigger Chinese firms and banks where the business language is English there seems no valid reason why Malays could not be employed. Perhaps they do not work as hard as non-Malays. There seems to be some basis for this accusation, but again it cannot be as bad as it is made out. Government departments and a number of British firms have survived with Malay employees. It is unreasonable to put all the Malays into one category and label them as lazy. A more liberal and understanding attitude is needed. In time there should emerge a core of adjusted Malays whose ability to work and whose knowledge of business and related subjects should be almost, if not quite equal to that of the non-Malays. Even now there are Malays who have proved themselves better than average in the fields they have managed to penetrate.

Races are differentiated not merely by ethnic origin, but also by many other characteristics. These characteristics are important. How these characteristics develop is another matter, but when races compete in a given field, these characteristics play an extremely important role. The Jews for example are not merely hook-nosed, but understand money instinctively. The Europeans are not only fair-skinned, but have an insatiable curiosity. The Malays are not merely brown, but are also easy-going and tolerant. And the Chinese are not just almond-eyed people, but are also inherently good businessmen. Their progress in the whole of Southeast Asia will testify to this.

Such characteristics differentiate races much more than the physical factors of colour and physiognomy. All these characteristics are, of course, found in all races to a greater or lesser degree. The possession of these characteristics means little until different races come into contact with each other. Jewish stinginess and financial wizardry gained them the commercial control of Europe and provoked an anti-Semitism which waxed and waned throughout Europe through the ages. European curiosity and hunger for new experiences led to the European exploration and conquest of lands belonging to the less curious people of Africa and Asia. Malay *laissez faire* and tolerance permitted the British conquest of Malaya without formal war and the subsequent influx of non-Malay Asians. Chinese business acumen made the Chinese the universal middlemen of Southeast Asia. It can be seen that these characteristics determine the relationship between races when they come in contact with each other. Within the same race these characteristics are of no great importance as they do not give undue advantage or handicap anyone. But the moment different races come into contact with each other, these

84

characteristics immediately make themselves felt and emphasize ethnic differences.

This little digression is essential to the further discussion of racial inequality and its meaning in Malaysia. It explains why the Malays are rural and economically backward, and why the non-Malays are urban and economically advanced. It is not the choice of the Malays that they should be rural and poor. It is the result of the clash of racial traits. They are easy-going and tolerant. The Chinese especially are hard-working and astute in business. When the two came in contact the result was inevitable. Before the onslaught of the predatory Chinese the Malays retreated to areas which were less attractive. The Government perceiving the result of this contest of racial characteristics hurriedly made Malay Reservation Laws which, while they do help the Malays, have also been instrumental in keeping the Malays rural.

Matters would have rested there but for the factors of education and politics. Things began to appear to the Malays in quite a different light. They, like everyone else, do not wish to be rural and poor. They want to be equal to the others in this country. They want to be urban, rich and educationally advanced. They want what they consider to be a fair share in the prosperity of this land of plenty. It is no good pointing out to them that the fault lies in their character. It is no good telling them that everything that can be done to help them has been done by the Government. Until they have a fair share, until there is racial equality, they cannot ignore or absolve other factors and practices which obstruct their quest for a place in the sun. To them it will always be discrimination in commerce and industry which is keeping them backward. They are not being given the chances which other independent people are getting. It is true that the Government is doing its best, but the Government alone cannot bring about racial equality. The people themselves must practise racial equality before it can become a fact. And to practise racial equality is to do away with discrimination in commerce and industry. This discrimination not only creates racial inequality but, by

85

banishing the Malay from the urban areas, actually perpetuates and emphasizes inequality.

How does keeping the Malays in rural areas perpetuate and emphasize racial inequality? I have pointed out how the city dweller is more sophisticated than the rural folk because of his variety of experience in the city. But experience and background are not the only thing which develop the urban dweller. A host of other factors are also directly and indirectly responsible.

The best schools are in the towns. In Malaya, despite every effort by the Government to give similar facilities to the rural areas, the fact still remains that the urban child has an infinitely greater chance of going to a good school than a rural child. The great names among schools are in bigger towns whose populations are almost exclusively non-Malay. Good teachers and good teaching facilities and aids are to be found in these schools. Naturally, these schools are expensive, and beyond the means of the majority of the Malays living in the towns and cities.

In Kuala Lumpur, Ipoh and Penang, the best schools are almost exclusively attended by non-Malays. Good schools are not created overnight. Good schools in the cities have traditions dating back over a hundred years. Their buildings are solid and spacious. The playgrounds are well-kept. The teachers are the best and most dedicated. And the yearly results demonstrate the superiority of the pupils to whom these schools are available. From these schools stream out students who have been, and will be, the privileged class of Malaysian society. They will be the doctors, lawyers, architects and other professional people. They will be the managers and entrepreneurs. They will be the leaders of the future. Aggressive, knowledgeable and well-versed in the ways of the world, they are well-equipped to shoulder aside their rural counterparts, even if the latter have equal paper qualifications.

From the schools, the problem continues into the colleges and the university. With the unequal educational background of the different communities it is not surprising that higher education should further emphasize and perpetuate racial inequality. The colleges and the University of Malaya claim a right to independence from political interference. They wish to have, and are granted the right to pick and choose their students without regard for the political needs of the country. They claim that as educational institutions their only concern is academic qualifications and standards. They do not care for racial origins. They do not discriminate. And the result looks like discrimination. The background of education, as we have pointed out, tends to favour the urban dwellers, and so by extension, the non-Malays. These are the people who year in and year out come up with the best results. These are the privileged people in the best primary and secondary schools. As a result, these very privileges lead them to even greater privileges in the colleges and universities.

In Malaysia there are more Malay primary school pupils than non-Malay. In the secondary schools this lead is cut, and there are slightly less Malay secondary school pupils, especially in the English stream. But in the higher educational institutions the pattern of racial inequality for the future is set. The colleges and the institutions at home and abroad have more non-Malays than Malays.

It may be argued that higher educational institutions cannot diverge from their purpose, their *raison d'etre*. Their interest is education, not racial problems. They only choose according to ability. Now let us examine other countries. Is educational ability the sole criterion for admission? Do local conditions have no influence on the intake into a college or university?

In the United States after the war, universities had to accept any war veteran who chose to enter any university. The basis for this discrimination in favour of the veterans was not just one of gratitude, but also because the war had handicapped the soldiers. The war had forced the soldiers to give up their normal education which would have taken at least some of them to the universities. As there was no means of distinguishing who these would have been, every veteran was treated as if he had the potential for higher education. There is no doubt that but for the fact of being war veterans, quite a number of these people would not have even got near a university. But the point is that having been accorded the opportunity, even some of the less promising had apparently made good. Is not this argument valid in Malaysia?

It is not the intention here to disparage other countries, but it is clear to anyone who cares to investigate, that academic standards in some countries, while they satisfy the minimum, are not very high. With independence for many countries, there has been a rash of new universities. These national universities cater for the needs of the new nations, and take into consideration the conditions existing within the countries. If the general standard of education in a new nation is low, then its national university will admit anyone able to make the grade. But if the standard is high then making the grade is not good enough. The potential students are not just those who make the grade, but those who have topped the grade. In other words, while there may be a lot of students with a sufficient basic education to profit from a university education, not all of them will be given the chance to further their studies.

It cannot be doubted that even those who barely make the grade can, with proper coaching, achieve high standards. The capacity for imbibing knowledge does not manifest itself evenly throughout life. Nor is the method of grading the learning potential of individuals infallible. It is entirely possible for even drop-outs to do better than the students most likely to succeed.

In the Congo before Independence there was hardly one university student. All were considered to have no potential. Indeed, the standards attained by the Congolese in primary and secondary education did not indicate a capacity for further studies. Since Independence in the Congo, their national university, and even foreign universities, have accepted Congolese students with lower grades than normally required by universities. In the past few years the number of Congolese with university degrees has increased by leaps and bounds. And yet if a strict adherence to standards were to be kept, these Congolese would have been denied higher education. Indeed, if admission to universities were to be on a basis of competitive examination, with, say, their former colonial masters, there might not be any Congolese today with a university education. Here is a case of tailoring higher education to the needs of, and to the conditions prevailing in a given country.

Let us now consider the situation in Malaysia. Malaysia is a uniquely multiracial country. Even the Negroes of America are more easily integrated with the whites than are the different races in Malaysia integrated among themselves. The Negroes are Christians, they speak the same language and have basically the same customs as the whites. Intermarriage occurs and has always occurred. But in Malaysia the division is not merely ethnic, cultural, lingual and economic but, as we have seen, also educational. The Malays being rural and poor get fewer opportunities for good primary and secondary education than the non-Malays who are rich and urban. Every year the examination results show the acute disparity between the races. And despite all efforts, the effect of generations of different experiences and backgrounds cannot be completely eradicated to result in equal opportunities for the development of the races. For years to come the average higher educational qualifications of the Malays are going to lag behind those of other races. Under these circumstances the usual competition between applicants for entry into the universities and colleges at home and abroad are going to work to the disadvantage of the Malays. In every course of study, if the places available are less than the number of applicants, the Malays will either not be admitted, or only a few of them will be admitted. The bigger the difference between available places and number of applicants, the smaller will be the chance for the Malays to obtain admittance. And the less chance they have to better their lot, the less will be their chance of urbanizing. And as I have pointed out, the less urban the Malays are, the greater the inequality between races will be.

As an illustration, a look at the Faculty of Medicine should suffice. Every year there are a limited number of places in the University of Malaya for courses leading to a medical degree. Every year the best students in the country apply to study medicine. Every one of these students has to have the basic minimum qualification to become a doctor. Experience everywhere has shown that students with these minimum qualifications who are accepted into the Medical Faculty will, given the proper training, eventually graduate as doctors. But because of limited places, only the very best are accepted. And because the Malay students, usually from the rural areas, or from inferior urban schools, have on the average poorer results, the chances are that only a very few will have sufficiently brilliant results to be among the best students selected for medical training. The competition for medical training will always work to the disadvantage of the Malays in this country. If they did not have the non-Malays to compete with, all the Malay applicants would have been accepted. But the non-Malay students with better examination results obtained through better schooling and background take up all available vacancies, and so bar the Malays from producing enough doctors in proportion to the percentage of the population they make up. In passing, it is worth mentioning that of the unsuccessful candidates for the University of Malaya, a good proportion of non-Malays go on to study medicine in India and other countries because their financial position enables them to do so. This of course increases the inequality in the number of doctors in each community.

What happens in the Medical Faculty also happens in other courses leading to the professions. Even in the Arts stream fewer Malays get places than non-Malays. Thus the gulf in education between Malays and non-Malays tends to widen, because those responsible for higher education believe that the realities of politics and the social make-up of the country have nothing to do with the so-called pursuit of knowledge.

And so education, instead of being an instrument for achieving racial equality, perpetuates, and even accentuates racial inequality. Poverty and lack of urban jobs make the Malays rural. Being rural and poor, the primary and secondary education of the Malays fall behind that of non-Malays. Poor secondary education bars the Malays from higher studies and the better jobs and professions which such studies make available. Lack of jobs in the professions banishes the Malays to the rural areas and to poverty, which in turn leads to poor education. This becomes a vicious circle.

Employment opportunities for the Malays are limited because of the discrimination in commercial and business circles controlled by non-Malays. In Government service there is no such discrimination. But the poor education of the Malays has not been taken into account within this non-discriminatory exercise. The reason why there are more non-Malays than Malays in Divisions I and II of Government service is again because education is a limiting factor. And this happens despite the four to one quota in favour of Malays in the Civil Service.

Technical and professional education for the Malays is very much behind that of the other communities. This has not always been so. In Kedah before the war there were more Malay engineering students in all grades than there were non-Malays. In fact, had the plan of the Kedah Government not been interrupted by the war, Malays would have taken over all the engineering posts held by Europeans in the Kedah Public Works Department.

After the war the position of the Malays was reversed. The doors of Government service were opened wide to non-Malays, and they, with their better education, soon acquired the necessary qualifications for filling up the new jobs created by the rapid progress of Malaya after the war. Thus we see that while the top posts are held by Malays, the majority of the rest are held by non-Malays. In time the normal process of retirement would completely eliminate the Malays who are now in the top posts.

As the majority of Division I and II posts are technical, the proportion of Malays occupying these positions is far smaller than the percentage of the population they make up. A study of trends would indicate that this proportion could be further reduced.

But what about the lower grades of Government service? Surely there would be sufficient qualified Malays to fill a fair proportion of these posts. No figures are available from the Government, but a study of the education service and the medical service should be illuminating.

One of the achievements of independent Malaysia is the great expansion of the education service. To cater for this a variety of institutions were established to train teachers rapidly. The Government continued to run Kirby College and Brinsford Lodge Teachers Training College on an expanded scale after *merdeka*, at the same time starting Day Training Centres and new teacher training schools in Malaya.

Except for the Sultan Idris Training College and the Malay Women Training College, Malacca, the other teachers' training institutions were open to all races. Every year there is a rush of qualified candidates for these colleges. Because the number of students with high grades among non-Malays exceeds the number of places and scholarships for higher studies, there are numerous over-qualified non-Malay applicants among those applying for teacher training. The effect of this spillover is to lessen the chances of those with only adequate qualification. As the few well qualified Malays would have found work elsewhere, the result is that few Malays get admitted into teacher training colleges or even the Day Training Centres because the majority of them have only minimum qualifications which cannot stand up to the over-qualified non-Malay applicants.

Over the years the effect of this so-called merit selection has been to make the teaching staff in schools other than the Malay vernacular schools (mis-named National Schools), more and more a non-Malay preserve. The trend continues so that even the Division III posts mirror the growing inequality of opportunities for Malays. A glance at the annual examination results will show why this has been and will continue to be so. And we know already the causes of poor results among the Malays in education. The vicious circle operates with predictable results in the education service too.

The nursing service used to have only one category. This category started with student nurses who, on completing their training, become qualified nurses eligible for promotion right up to the rank of Principle Matron. During the British regime this was only in theory, but now it is a fact.

From the beginning the nursing service had very few Malays. There was no discrimination against them, but their own prejudice and the small number of Malay girls gaining the basic qualification prevented Malays from entering the nursing service. In the post-war years most prejudice was overcome. But the number of Malay girls with the requisite qualification was still too small for them to make inroads into the service.

Some time before *merdeka* it was decided to create a new category of nurses of a lower grade. These assistant nurses as they were called did not need to have the same entrance qualification as ordinary nurses, and this resulted in a number of Malay girls becoming eligible to join the new service. But their modest debut was short-lived.

As the number of vacancies in the ordinary nursing service was inadequate to cope with the ever-growing number of non-Malay girls with the necessary qualifications, there was again a spillover which inundated the assistant-nursing service with over-qualified applicants. In time there were so many of these, that the lowering of qualifications failed to have the effect of enabling the less qualified Malays to become assistant nurses. The intake now is often in the proportion of one Malay to twenty non-Malays.

And so even in these Division IV posts the opportunities for the Malays are closing. What can be said of the assistant nurses can also be said of numerous other categories of Government employees. Competition based on so-called merit is gradually but surely squeezing the Malays out of every avenue of employment in Government service. The degree of the exclusion of Malays varies at present between the different states. The former Unfederated Malay states still manage to have a fair proportion of Malays. The proportion of Malays is lower in the former Federated Malay

States and is lowest in the former Straits Settlements. But the mobility of applicants after the states were fused into a union meant that the states with a large Malay population could not long keep out the non-Malays. It can be assumed that in time the lack of opportunity for the Malays will be uniform throughout West Malaysia.

There are still a few jobs where Malays can seek refuge. The rank and file of the armed forces and the police is one such place. The special "agencies" for the *bumiputera* like Majlis Amanah Ra'ayat, Federal Agricultural Marketing Authority and Bank Bumiputera still openly dare to show preference for the Malays. And there is of course that picturesque group which makes Government offices in Kuala Lumpur so Malay — the office-boys in their abbreviated Malay national costume.

What has been described is obvious and basic. From these inequalities of opportunity spring other inequalities, such as the miserable houses of the Malays compared to the houses of the non-Malays, the poor health of the Malays against the vigour of the non-Malays, the high death and infant mortality rates of the Malays compared to non-Malays, the lack of savings and capital of the Malays when compared to non-Malays.

The list is endless. The obstacles of unequal opportunities emphasize and multiply every inequality existing between Malays and non-Malays. And the worst of this inequality is the inequality of self-expression. Poorly educated, traditionally polite or hamstrung by their lack of independence in employment, the Malays cannot even state their case clearly. Tongue-tied they watch in dismay as others accuse them, who already have so little, of denying opportunities to others, of practising discrimination against non-Malays and of domination in politics. How ridiculous the accusations against them are is shown by one of the most significant of recent events. One of the most prosperous manufacturing firms in Malaysia produces cigarettes bearing the name of a well-known London firm. In order to demonstrate that it is in accord with Government wishes, this foreign company appointed a Malay as Chairman of its board of directors, and also took in a small number of Malays to work as gardeners, drivers and unskilled factory workers. The majority of the firm's employees ranging from executive officers, clerks and skilled workers were non-Malays.

Suddenly a rumour was started that the factory had sacked Chinese employees and replaced them with Malays. Without waiting to confirm the truth of this rumour the retailers of this firm's cigarettes, ninety-five per cent of whom are Chinese, initiated a boycott. Apparently no actual directive was given by any responsible organization. By word of mouth the boycott was spread throughout the length and breadth of Malaya. In a week this firm felt the pinch. Before a month was out the situation had become so bad that the company was forced to seek the aid of Chinese distributors and the Chinese Chambers of Commerce. The firm was forced to submit to an inspection by group after group of Chinese before it was admitted that there was no truth in the allegation and the boycott was called off.

One would have thought that the Malays would have protested at what was blatantly an anti-Malay attitude. But there was not a squeak as the rule that Chinese may not be replaced by Malays under any condition has apparently been established. The victory for the Chinese was complete. Henceforth factories and other enterprises must be extremely careful not to annoy the Chinese if they want their business to remain healthy.

The only basis for racial harmony in a multiracial society is racial equality. To establish racial equality it is necessary to understand what racial equality means. In Malaysia the fact that every community feels that it is being discriminated against is proof that racial equality is not very well understood.

The Malay case has been stated at length. For the non-Malays the basis of their discontent and resentment is the presence of laws and policies which, by seeming to favour the Malays, appear to make second class citizens of non-Malays. Assuming that these laws are what the non-Malays think they are, they must be considered very flimsy barriers indeed to racial equality and harmony. It takes but a few scraps of paper and some "ayes" in the appropriate legislative body to right the alleged wrongs.

But will repealing these laws magically bring forth racial equality and harmony in Malaysia? If what has been said here is even remotely correct, it must appear that repealing the so-called discriminatory laws will not only fail to create racial equality, but it will in fact deepen the the cleavage and the disparity between races. For the basis of the Malay claim to discrimination is not man-made laws but inherent human behaviour.

It has been pointed out that races are not only distinguished by colour, physiognomy, language and culture, but also by their character. Inherent racial character explains the rapid recovery of Germany and Japan after their defeat in World War II. Racial character explains the mild treatment of the Germans and the Japanese by the British victors of this war despite atrocities committed by the former during the war. The development of South America lags behind that of North America despite equally rich resources because the Southern European who colonized South America differs in behaviour and character from the Northern European who colonized North America. The gleaming success of South Africa as compared with the other African countries is a product of the different racial character of the immigrant white African and the indigenous black African.

Racial character and behaviour cannot be changed overnight by man-made laws. However, changes in racial character and behaviour are not impossible. The medieval code of ethics for example is not the same as it is now. Religious tolerance, once almost unknown in many countries, is now prevalent almost everywhere. Even the Russian Communists, once dedicated to world Communism through fair means or foul, are now less aggressive and have accepted co-existence instead. The different and often antagonistic white races which emigrated to the United States have so changed that they have characters which can be described as typically American and which differ very much from those of their diverse European origins.

Human racial character can change, but it takes time for human beings to adjust. Change also needs incentives and a favourable atmosphere.

The Malay claim to being discriminated against in Malaysia is based not on laws but on the character and behaviour of the major racial groups in Malaysia. The Malays are spiritually inclined, tolerant and easy-going. The non-Malays and especially the Chinese are materialistic, aggressive and have an appetite for work. For equality to come about it is necessary that these strikingly contrasting races adjust to each other. Laws cannot do this. Only understanding, goodwill and time can. And understanding and goodwill can only come about in time if the meaning of racial equality is understood by all concerned.

6: The Bases of National Unity

National unity, like most political terms, is interpreted differently by different people. Like justice, it is a universal concept. It cannot be uniquely interpreted by or for one community alone. It must have certain values which are common although variations are permissible under differing circumstances.

Today there is a Department of National Unity in Malaysia. This is a measure of the recognition that national unity has gained not only in the eyes of the National Operations Council Government but also of right-thinking people in Malaysia.

The basis of national unity, simply stated, is a single ethnic group possessing a common language, culture and religion confined within an area of definite geographical boundaries. All these factors when present together have never failed to create a nation in the old sense of the word.

In the days when communication was poor and travelling minimal, nations were merely extensions of tribal organizations which in turn were extensions of combined or extended families. The limiting factor was geographical barriers, be it distance, mountains, the sea or rivers. Within a defined area, tribes came together in peace or war through the development of a common language, culture and religion and fused to become a nation.

The sense of loyalty and unity within a nation was brought about by the ability to understand a common language, culture and religion. When other racial groups with differing cultures etc. came in contact with a given group the inability to understand each other led to conflict. In armed conflict a keener sense of kinship was felt within each group which led to a stronger sense of national unity.

In modern times, the United States of America became a great experiment in nation-building. When the thirteen colonies gained independence they proved that kings were

98

not important in uniting people. After gaining independence, the settlers of Anglo-Saxon stock began admitting immigrants of different ethnic and racial stocks with different religions, cultures and languages. The question was whether the adoption and not the inheritance of a common language and culture could create loyalty to a given legal state. The United States is of course a legal state, not a natural state with natural geographical barriers as boundaries.

During the period of intensive immigration to the United States in the nineteenth and early twentieth centuries, the new nation was severely tested. New immigrants ranged from Chinese to Russians. Practically every ethnic and language group was included. Knowledge of English, the official language among immigrants was minimal or nil, as was knowledge of the culture and historical background of the United States. Religions were equally diverse. Out of this polyglot mixture of people, national unity was built primarily on a basis of language. The thirteen colonies were settled by people who spoke English, and they and their descendants were the core of the nation. Here an important principle was established and upheld — immigrants wishing to be nationals had to learn English as the national language and its acceptance had to be complete, and the language actually spoken in everyday life. There was no question of saying "We accept English as the official language of the United States", and then ignoring it. Much less was there any suggestion that immigrant languages should be placed anywhere near English or even officially tolerated. Indeed, it was a condition of citizenship, implied through loyalty to the constitution, that new citizens of non-Anglo Saxon origin did not have the right to insist on the parity of any other language with English. So well was this understood that although large pockets of non-Anglo Saxon stock are concentrated in certain areas, no attempt is made to perpetuate their own language. In most instances their own languages were lost after one generation.

Having created a society in which the people literally understood each other, a national culture was allowed to develop freely. But because language is so inextricably tied with culture, the result was a mainly Anglo-Saxon culture, distinct in its ability to accept modified non-British influences. In this way national unity was achieved without need for a common ethnic origin, geographical barriers and religion. However certain auxiliary controls were used. Education is almost exclusively in English. History is confined to American history with the origin of the British colonies given more emphasis than the historical backgrounds of the later immigrants. To create a sense of loyalty to a state without hereditary kings and with boundaries which are not natural barriers, respect for the constitution, the flag and other symbols of nationhood are taught in schools and wherever citizens meet.

The acid test of American national unity came with the two major wars fought by the United States. It was inevitable that at least some Americans would have to fight people of the same ethnic group as their progenitors. Would their identity with America be strong enough to make them fight with and kill people who were actually their former countrymen? The answer was clear when General Eisenhower, himself of German stock, led the United States and the Western Allies to victory.

The American experiment of nation-building was repeated with apparent success in the Latin American countries and in Australia. To these countries, as to the United States, people of various races emigrated, accepted and used the established language, learnt to respect the symbols of nationhood, and became a united people, recognizable and internationally distinctive. Language thus seems to be the key to national unity. It opens the door to a basic culture, and through a unified education system, to other essential symbols of unity such as the constitution, the flag, the anthem and the laws of the country.

But this emphasis on language as a unifying force provokes the retort that Switzerland has proved that a single national language is not essential for national unity. Those who cite Switzerland as an example ignore quite a number of things that are unique to the Swiss and to Switzerland.

Switzerland is held together not so much by internal unity as by the forces outside, the nations around her, for whom Switzerland acts as a buffer, an outlet and neutral ground during disputes. For Switzerland there can only be one role — neutrality. The excitement of power politics and wars is not for her.

Internally the wealth of Switzerland lies in the skill of her people and the political calm that lures tourists. These things prosper most when politics have the least influence. Thus, for both external and internal reasons the Swiss abhor politics. At a recent general election hardly anybody contested or voted, and the same government has remained in power simply because no one has been interested in politics. In this atmosphere language cannot become a political issue. It can neither unite or divide.

Another remarkable thing about the Swiss is that it is possible for them to have four official languages. Of these Romansch is confined to such a small community (one-third of the population of the canton of Graubauden), that for practical purposes there are only three official languages — French, Italian and German. Practically every adult Swiss speaks at least two of these three official languages. What this means is that a situation can hardly ever arise where a Swiss cannot understand another Swiss. Besides, French and Italian belong to one language group, and it takes but little learning for one group to understand the other.

Finally the Swiss are all Europeans — the French and Italian speaking being of Latin origin, and the German speaking being Teutonic. All groups being of a European culture which is almost uniform, they found no difficulty in blending in Switzerland. In these circumstances language becomes an insignificant factor in national unity. Too many things are common and too many forces within and without are conducive to unity, so that the fact that four languages are official means nothing at all.

To recapitulate, we can say that originally the bases of national unity are a confined land peopled by ethnically, culturally, linguistically and religiously similar people. The course of modern history has however shown that ethnic origins and religions are not indispensable. Language and an intimately related culture remain essential factors in the establishment of national unity. In a multiracial nation like Malaysia, unity can, therefore, be achieved provided agreement can be reached as to the choice of language and the related culture. Provided the chosen language is accepted, a multiracial nation can mould a national unity by employing accessory methods such as the projection of a focus of loyalty like a king, the teaching of national history, the veneration of national symbols in the form of the flag, the anthem, the colours etc., and last but not least, respect for the constitution and laws of the country. During all these processes, the people must truly integrate. Every barrier which tends to distinguish between racial, ethnic or other origins must be broken. Discrimination in all walks of life must be eliminated. And finally, inter-racial marriages should be encouraged. These are the bases of national unity, the understanding of which is the *sine qua non* of a multiracial society desirous of building a stable and viable nation.

7: Rehabilitation of the Malays and the Malay Dilemma

The Malay dilemma is not merely economic but political as well. Today everyone talks of the relationship between racial friction and the unequal development of the different races in Malaysia. At one time it was thought that the best way to treat this disparity was to ignore it. Some even believed that there was no dilemma because the Malays had no wish to be anything but their modest selves.

The events of 13 May 1969 have shown that facts, however unpleasant, must be faced. The people who ran *amok* on that fateful day were Malays. That sudden outburst has undone almost all that has been achieved over the past twelve years. If we are not to see a repetition of this carnage, it would be as well to know some of the reasons for that unprecedented calamity, and to think seriously about rehabilitating the Malays.

For the Malay dilemma is also a Malaysian dilemma. The Malaysian nation cannot expect to thrive and prosper with this cancer eating away at its heart. The Malays form a substantial portion of the population and anything affecting them must affect the nation. It is therefore imperative that a determined attempt be made to solve this dilemma. The first need is a revolution. Revolution is a word which is unduly feared in Malaysia. Revolution creates visions of assassinations and anarchy. But revolutions can be creative and orderly if the mechanics are understood by those best able to carry them through.

The alternative is evolution. Evolution cannot be properly controlled in speed or in objective. It depends far too much on circumstances and a multitude of factors difficult to detect and therefore difficult to utilize and control. If revolution is to be the solution to the Malay problem in Malaysia, it must be a carefully planned revolution; it must be enlightened and it must avoid the pitfalls and mistakes of other revolutions. This is where an analysis of the Malay character, culture and abilities is useful.

Revolution implies drastic changes. Doctrinaire revolutionists often fail because they see only the objective and entirely disregard circumstances, established forces and institutions. For a revolution to succeed in Malaysia, it is essential that we recognize what can be done away with and what must remain and even be propagated. The object is the betterment of the Malays and not the destruction of others. Malays can be made to take their proper place in Malaysian society without having to displace others.

The first thing that comes to mind is that the vast majority of Malays are feudalist and wish to remain so. A revolution which starts off by preaching the destruction of the established monarchical order will therefore fail. It will not win the support of the majority of orthodox Malays. In any case, the monarchy has done no real harm to the Malays or to anyone else. The maintenance of the system is no doubt costly, but being separated from power, the rulers cannot constitute a tyranny. Besides a Malaya without rulers would mean the complete eclipse of the Malays. It is the rulers who have in the past furnished, and continue to present the Malay character of Malaya, Remove them, and the last vestige of traditional Malaya would disappear. This is why Malays have remained feudalist despite their new education and political sophistication. It is essential therefore that the monarchy remains. As constitutional monarchs, the sultans are enlightened and aware of the changing times. They have not really got in the way of progress. If the changes proposed are for the good of the country and the Malays, the sultans will not stand in the way. Indeed, in the quest for Independence the consent of the rulers paved the way for a smooth transition and avoided the bitter recriminations so common elsewhere.

Religion is another established force with the Malays. No change, no plan and no ideology which runs counter to the religion of the Malays can succeed. Islam must therefore be left alone in the quest for Malay progress. In fact,

104

Islam must be upheld and even further propagated if success is to be assured.

The third force with the Malays is their traditional custom or *adat* derived from their system of values. But *adat* is no longer the essential thing it once was. *Adat* is losing its grip on the Malays. No longer is it said that "It is far better that our children die rather than our *adat* ". *Adat* therefore can be changed or ignored in the process of progress. The revolution should consider *adat* but should not be unduly bound by it.

Having evaluated and accepted the established forces, the future of the Malays can be mapped out. It must be emphasized that no plan can be complete. There will be defects and omissions. There will even be mistakes. The important thing is to realize the need for a revolutionary plan and its early and thorough implementation.

Essentially because of environmental and hereditary factors, the Malays have become a rural race with only a minute portion of them in the towns. Rural people everywhere are less sophisticated and progressive than urban people. Our solution to this problem must be to attempt a reversal of this state of affairs. In other words, we must seek to urbanize the Malays.

There will be many objections to this, but all objections must wither in the face of the acute shortage of arable land in places where there is the most number of Malays. Relocation and resettlement will solve this for one generation, but Muslim inheritance laws will reduce such settlements into uneconomic holdings as soon as the settlers die. Too many small plots of land are being held and cultivated by too many people, mostly without proper legal titles, as the beneficiaries struggle endlessly with the intricacies of inheritance laws.

The problems of urbanization are many and varied. But unlike those in other countries, these problems cannot be left to resolve themselves. They must be overcome systematically by Government planning. Since the Malays are traditionally a rural people, they do not gravitate to the towns to the degree that other races do. It is imperative that they be induced positively to come to the towns. And the only inducement that could convince them is the security of regular incomes.

Malaya is spending large sums of money on development. Bridges, roads, buildings, factories and other projects are constantly being built. Most of these construction jobs are being let out on contracts. The Government, through the Jabatan Kerja Raya, merely supervises. Big contractors in Malaya are either Chinese or Europeans. There are a few small Malay contractors. But the Jabatan Kerja Raya time and standard stipulations mean that it is safer for contractors to exclude Malay workers even in unskilled work. Now if the Government should insist on gradually undertaking a greater proportion of development projects itself, it should be possible for Malays from the rural areas to be employed in increasing numbers. Starting with unskilled labour they can gradually progress to semi-skilled and finally skilled work. They will learn through practice while receiving pay. This is important. The Malays must acquire skills through working. They must not be subjected to theoretical lessons. In an experiment to teach skills to Malay youths in rural continuation schools, the result was a failure because these youths knew that there was no future for them. Even if they become skilled in bricklaying, no one would employ them because of racial prejudice. On the other hand, construction firms forced by the Government to employ Malay workers have found them entirely capable of acquiring the necessary skills. In this scheme employment is assured and training comes later. If sufficient inducement is offered for skills acquired, the abilities of Malay craftsmen will get a chance to be used and developed.

But security of employment must not be so rigidly ensured as to kill enterprise. The system of pensions which is now taken for granted in Government service has tied the Malays to the Government. Malays in Government service are usually more knowledgeable and capable than Malays employed elsewhere. This is not an accident, but the result of the Government having a choice of the best through the salaries offered. Besides, work in Government service gives them an insight into the intricacies of official procedures which is an advantage in business. They would, after some years in Government service, be the best people to go out and work in competition with non-Malays. But Malays in Government service will never leave the service because of the security of a pension. Even when they realize that they have sufficient knowledge and experience to earn much more on their own in other types of work, the thought of losing their pension rights prevents them from leaving Government service.

This was noticed in the field of politics. When the nation needed capable Malay leaders it was realized that most of them were to be found in Government service. They would not leave Government service because of the security it offered. It was not until a scheme was worked out whereby they could retain their pensions that they were induced to enter the political arena.

Similarly, in the scheme to employ Malays and train them in skilled and semi-skilled work on Government projects, the restrictive influence of pensions must not be permitted. The Malays must be made to realize that work with the Government is merely a stepping stone to better things. Once skill has been acquired they should not hesitate to go elsewhere for better employment. In fact they should be encouraged to do so. Provisions for a provident fund however do not have the same effect as pensions. If security in old age is morally necessary then it should take the form of a provident fund. The advantage of this lies in the fact that it follows the employee wherever he goes. It does not tie him to one employer for the whole of his working life as a pension does.

The security of a regular salary however small will attract Malays to work. The aim should be not so much to employ them permanently, as to accustom them to do work other than planting padi and to urbanize them. The salary offered is thus of great importance. It should be higher than the average Malay income from padi farming, after taking into consideration the low cost of living in the *kampongs* and the tolerant attitude of Malays towards unemployed relatives. But ideally the salary should not be such as to make them hesitant about leaving these jobs to take up similar but better-paid employment elsewhere.

Trade unionism has come to stay in Malaya. It is generally regarded as good for the workers. It prevents exploitation of labour and enables workers to have a fair share of the prosperity which is partly the product of their labour. Unfortunately some workers, glorifying in their new-found strength, see in trade unions not only the opportunity to use collective bargaining for better wages but for making other demands. No disciplinary action can be taken without costly industrial action. Under such conditions diligence is not encouraged and the desire for self-improvement is inhibited. In a scheme to force Malay labour into the competitive field of skilled and semi-skilled work, trade unionism can find no place. Absolute security and good working conditions are not the aims of this scheme. Trade unions are therefore superfluous. To ensure that workers may get a fair deal, and nepotism and other forms of favouritism are avoided, an impartial body should be set up to look after the welfare of workers.

Wherever there is an influx of workers into urban areas, slums mushroom. As the idea in urbanizing the Malays is to provide them with the facilities and sophistication of the towns, allowing them to live in slum conditions would defeat the purpose. It is essential that low cost houses be built to accommodate them. The benefit of the newly urbanized rural dwellers would be maximal if small, self-contained satellite towns are built. There should be shops, markets, schools, community centres and health facilities.

I have already referred to the benefits the Malays can derive from contact with non-Malays. These satellite towns would be the first place where this contact could be made. An important feature of these new communities must be the provision of facilities for coming into contact with non-Malays. A proportion of the houses and shops should be for non-Malays. The staff employed to run public utilities must also have a fair sprinkling of non-Malays. But contact should be controlled because there is always a tendency for non-Malays to swamp the Malays, especially in markets and shops. Facilities for petty trading should be an incentive for Malays to urbanize.

In the past the Chinese effectively excluded the Malays from all forms of business. The reasons why this happened are fairly well known. Those which concern racial characteristics are difficult to overcome. Indeed the only way is to urbanize the Malays. But we cannot wait for this to happen before the Malays reap the rewards which come with trading, on no matter how small a scale.

Consequently, protection must be initially afforded the Malay shopkeepers. Most of the shops and markets in the new satellite towns must be allocated to Malays. But this alone is not enough. In order that the new urban dwellers patronize their own community shops, conditions must be created which will make it difficult or costly for them to buy elsewhere. Cooperative shops would, in theory, induce members to patronize their own shops. In practice, cooperative shops have failed with the Malays. The dividends paid by such shops, even when properly run, are minimal and only come once a year. Malays as a rule are impatient and are more attracted by immediate benefits. Competitive prices and easy credit offered by privately run Chinese shops constitute such a temptation that Malay customers would desert their own cooperative shop. Cooperatives can be dismissed as a means of promoting Malay participation in petty trading, and of controlling the drain on Malay income.

A minor but important factor which may help Malay shopkeeping is to utilize the natural industry and shrewdness of Malay women. Among padi planters, the men work roughly two months in the year. The women toil throughout the year. They are concerned with padi-planting as much as the men. In addition, during the planting and harvesting seasons, they cook for all the farm-hands. When work on the *bendangs* is over, they continue with household work, look after the children and busy themselves with a host of other minor but essential work. In some instances the women make cakes to earn extra money and even peddle clothing and sell forest produce. Preparing salted fish and pickling fresh-water fish are also done exclusively by women. Malay women are more diligent and shrewd than Malay men. Malay women have a greater tendency to save than men. This is seen in their partiality towards buying jewellery rather than other less permanent luxuries.

In the urbanization scheme, the men would be required to work at salaried jobs. The women, even if occupied with household work, could still find time to mind little shops. The essential thing is that the shop and dwelling should be in the same building. In Kelantan, Malay village shops are invariably the front of the owners' houses, and are minded almost exclusively by women. Indeed most petty trading and hawking is done by women in Kelantan. Nevertheless all these safeguards and planning would fail if competition by the more thrifty and astute Chinese petty shopkeepers is not minimized. We know that before the Chinese came to Malaya, the Malays had been shopkeepers and petty traders. It was because of the superiority of Chinese business tactics that Malay shops have disappeared.

There are many facets to Chinese business skill. The basis is the natural Chinese thriftiness which allows them to save and to expand on a minimal profit. The Malays can be told to spend less, but habit and the character of generations cannot be removed in a single stroke. There are also various tactics the Chinese use which can be circumvented to allow Malay shopkeepers a chance to compete fairly. One of these is casual credit. More shrewd in their judgement of character, the Chinese allow a certain amount of credit which ties their customers to them. Cash advances are not excluded from these tactics. In the *kampongs* this has been developed into the unscrupulous *padi-kuncha* system. An end to this practice must be instituted through legislation. Sales must be cash, or if credit is granted, a proper account must be kept which must be open for inspection by tax officials. Excessive accumulative credits must not be allowed. Liability must always be directed at the shopkeeper so that he stands to lose all from the practice of putting his customers under obligation. In this way the petty loans to Malay customers would not be used to keep them from buying from any shop.

The one single factor most responsible for pushing the Malays out of petty trading is the pricing of merchandise. East of Suez prices are never fixed. Bargaining is an accepted procedure. Buying is a process of haggling, a contest between customer and shopkeeper. It is always taken for granted that the merchant never loses on any transaction. This is not always true. Quite often the merchant agrees to a price which is below his cost in order to profit on less tangible things. Goodwill is an important commodity in trade. If, by losing a few cents, the merchant is ensured of further sales to the same customer, he will have no hesitation about foregoing his immediate gain. If competition with neighbouring shops is involved then the decision to lose now and gain later is even easier to make. With their thrift and their relatively bigger capital the Chinese shopkeepers can afford to lose more frequently than the Malays; or they can make a lower margin of profit which will also ensure continued patronage by their customers.

If the Malays are to be brought back into petty trading the flexible price system must be abolished. If all merchandise sold by all shops had fixed prices clearly displayed, and if sale below the displayed prices were prohibited. cut-throat competition would be eliminated. The customer would not have a choice of prices in any given locality and would buy from various shops. In these circumstances the Malay shop next to a Chinese shop would not be squeezed out of business. He would not be accused of secretly selling at a higher price, and his ability to haggle with his customer would not be put to the test every time a sale is made. But of course there would always be means to counter price-fixing of this nature. Difference in wholesale prices might affect the actual profit of the retailer. This could be overcome by spot-checks, by insistence on receipts and by actual price-fixing for wholesale deals which would have to be receipted and accounted for in returns of income. Weighing machines too should be changed by law so that spring balances are exclusively used. The present use of the moveable counter-weight balances called *daching* can easily be manipulated to give short weights. The small-time Chinese retailer is adept at this practice and unscrupulous enough to use it as a weapon in competition.

These are but two methods which could be used to counter price-fixing and price-displaying. A sharp lookout must always be kept for attempts to by-pass these methods of minimizing unfair competition. Of course this suggestion should not be limited to the schemes of resettling rural people in urban areas. It should be applied throughout the nation so that fair competition would be the norm instead of the exception.

It is impossible to map out here all the steps which could be taken to urbanize the Malays. The intention is merely to show that it is beneficial and it can be done. Properly regulated and planned, urbanization appears to afford the only method of keeping the Malays abreast of developments around them and in the rest of the world. It would also make available to them the modern facilities of the towns which no amount of good intentions could bring to the rural areas. Their health, education and outlook would literally change without conscious effort.

On the other hand, the present ideas about keeping the Malays in the rural areas in order that they do not swell the ranks of the unemployed in the towns only means that we are refusing to recognize the grave problems of poverty and backwardness in the rural areas. Land hunger is as much a fact as land shortage. In one generation Muslim laws of inheritance alone will render all present holdings uneconomical. Already forest and other reserves have been occupied and cultivated by settlers prepared to defy the law. Only the towns with their industries and petty trading opportunities can absorb future unemployed Malays. And, in order that absorption is smooth and efficient, the necessary planning for urbanization must begin now. There is no other way out for the Malays or the Government.

Urbanization and forced acquisition of skilled labour cannot by themselves constitute a revolution, even in the context of Malay society. But they certainly represent a radical change. The fact of urbanization alone involves a process of physical and psychological uprooting of the Malays from the traditional rural society. There can be no doubt that with this uprooting, old values and ways of life must give way to new. It is the old values and ways of life which have held the Malays back, cutting them off from the changes continually taking place in the rest of the country and the world. One has but to compare the actual physical structure of Malay villages to appreciate how static their society is.

To complete the rehabilitation of the Malays there is a need for them to break away from custom or *adat* and to acquire new ways of thinking and a new system of values. Urbanization will do this to a certain extent, but there must also be a conscious effort to destroy the old ways and replace them with new ideas and values. The Malays must be confronted with the realities of life and forced to adjust their thinking to conform with these realities.

The Government has undertaken various programmes to help the progress of the Malays. Education has been stepped up and rural Malays have been given opportunities to tour the urban areas. But these are far from adequate. There is no systematic and co-ordinated orientation of the Malays towards progress. Above all, these piecemeal attempts to reorientate the Malays lack organization.

One of the things which illustrate how unadjusted the Malay mind is, is the frequent complaint against non-Malay employers. Malays working in non-Malay firms or under non-Malay superiors invariably complain that they are being discriminated against. What they do not seem able to understand is that this is completely natural. Non-Malays working under Malays feel the same way. But whereas non-Malays accept this as a matter of course, Malays fight tooth and nail against it. They do not try to ingratiate themselves with their superiors. They do not try to outshine the possible non-Malay competitors. They do not try to make themselves indispensable to their bosses. The result is that they invariably lose favour and their positions become untenable.

This inability to accept the inevitable represents a failure to adjust and adapt to circumstances. This particular inability is going to be a large obstacle in the near future when the graduates of the MARA Institute of Technology enter the field of commerce and industry. Malay or Malay controlled firms cannot absorb all these graduates. A majority of them will have to work directly under non-Malays. And this group is going to come up against the same problem of racial discrimination. Unless these young Malays understand this discrimination, they will find their positions untenable. If this happens then the Malays will fail again.

This is but one illustration of the failure of Malays to evaluate realities and adjust themselves. If the Malays are to be rehabilitated, all the attitudes and values that have contributed to their present dilemma must be studied, assessed and where necessary, discarded or modified.

Urbanization, acquisition of new skills and the acceptance by the Malays of new values which are still compatible with their religion and their basically feudal outlook, would constitute a revolution. Admittedly there is nothing new in these suggestions. All these things are indeed happening. But so far, the pace is a process of gentle evolution involving neither concerted action nor ruthlessness in implementation. The whole process must be planned and executed with speed and thoroughness to produce a complete and radical change in the Malays. If this revolution is brought about they would be rehabilitated and their dilemma would be over. The nation would be able to progress without the burden of a Malay problem.

8: The Malay Problem

In Malaysia, or more specifically in Malaya, the Malays are faced with a personal problem. It is a problem which concerns their real, innermost attitude towards Malaya and Malaysia, towards sharing the land of the Malays with others. It concerns their hopes when *merdeka* was achieved and the dashing of some of these hopes on the rocks of reality. It is a predicament which everyone has avoided mentioning in public for various reasons. The Chinese and Indians think that the Malays know that they have a perplexing problem and that public reference to it might start a chain reaction which could be uncontrollable and disastrous. The Malays themselves have shunned an open statement of the problem because it embarasses them, and is an embarassment to others. They, more than anyone else, have been responsible for keeping this peculiar Malay problem suppressed.

On the surface, the deliberate avoidance of discussion seems good. It preserves the atmosphere of tranquillity which is mistaken for racial harmony in Malaya. It makes for good administration. It encourages investment and development. But the actual situation beneath this seeming tranquillity and harmony is fraught with danger. Every community, whether Chinese, Indian or Malay, clinging tightly to racial loyalties, keeps on sparring with this Malay problem. And because each group does not know the other's strength, and the fierceness of the feelings involved, this sparring tends to build up tensions which could boil over. Should this happen, and it is very likely, the lack of mutual knowledge could make compromise impossible. The situation could become uncontrollable. There could be disaster. And what happened in Nigeria could be the fate of Malaya.

The fact that the Malays more than anyone else have caused the suppression of this problem is a paradox except

115

to those who understand the Malay character. It is important, therefore, that this peculiarity of the Malays be understood. It is an integral part of the problem. In fact it contributes to the magnitude and complexity of the problem. The Malay is courteous and self-effacing. His world is full of nobility and he is never far from his rajas and chiefs. He gives way and he shows them deference. It is good manners to do so. It is not degrading. It is in fact a mark of breeding. It is typical of the Malay to stand aside and let someone else pass. Not only does he stand aside, but he inclines himself in seeming obeisance. And the Malay who avails himself of this courtesy shows his breeding by not completely taking the path proferred. He too gives way and inclines himself. Each expects these little courtesies of the other. But this expectation stops as soon as the other party is not a Malay. The non-Malay is excused. He does not know. He is not to blame. The non-Malay is always privileged. He is not expected to conform. He can say and do things which would be considered rude or ill-mannered of a Malay. He can even conduct himself in the presence of the Malay's rajas and chiefs in a manner most unbecoming to a Malay, and get away with it. The fact that the Malay is prepared to forgive and tolerate the non-Malay on every occasion is in itself a mark of good breeding to him. It is bad manners to embarrass your guest and the non-Malay is always a guest to the Malay, a guest in his country.

But, unfortunately, what is merely good manners to the Malays is wrongly interpreted by non-Malays. The British consider the deference and the constant giving way on the part of the Malays as evidence of weakness and inferiority. The Malay habit of calling them *tuan* or "master" was taken as an acceptance that Europeans were in fact the master of the Malays.

Winstedt, in one of his English-Malay dictionaries, even went so far as to say that the correct way for Malays, including rajas, to address any European is to append the honorific *tuan* to the name. If this arrogance has never been openly resented or if the mistake has never been corrected, it was because the Malays considered it bad manners to correct mistakes in etiquette committed by foreigners.

The Chinese and Indians coming from countries with vast populations are less concerned about good behaviour and manners. In their lives, nobility which is always associated with breeding, was totally absent. Age and riches are the only things they defer to. The Chinese and Indians have never understood the Malay habit of giving way. They saw nothing in it which bespoke good breeding. They do not admire it and they have never felt the need to copy it. But they certainly found it to their advantage. They found that they do not have to conform, that they can get away with anything. They found to their advantage that they can do things which the Malay cannot. They found in fact that in the land of the Malays they are privileged.

The courtesy and the self-effacing habits of the Malays are but one aspect of the Malay character. The constant restraint the Malay imposes on himself is unnatural. There is always an internal struggle, a conflict, and this conflict finds expression in a variety of ways. The first and most important result is a withdrawing into himself and his race. He is never frank except with those whose sympathy he can rely on absolutely. And he can rely absolutely only on his own people. His opinions as expressed to those not of his own kind are therefore different from those expressed to his own kind. Of course the difference only occurs when what he has to express to others is unpleasant or unpalatable. Where his true opinion will cause no unpleasantness or animosity, he does not hesitate to voice it to his own community as well as other communities. It is, therefore, fallacious to accept the Malay at face value. It is far better if his politeness and his abhorrence of unpleasantness is understood for what they really are. The conflict within him is potentially dangerous. It is perpetually seeking expression.

Amok is a Malay word. It is a word now universally understood. There is no other single word that can quite describe *amok*. And the reason is obvious — for *amok* describes yet another facet of the Malay character. *Amok* represents the external physical expression of the conflict within the Malay which his perpetual observance of the rules and regulations of his life causes in him. It is a spilling over, an overflowing of his inner bitterness. It is a rupture of the bonds which bind him. It is a final and complete escape from reason and training. The strain and the restraint on him is lifted. Responsibility disappears. Nothing matters. He is free. The link with the past is severed, the future holds nothing more. Only the present matters. To use a hackneyed expression, he sees red. In a trance he lashes out indiscriminately. His timid, self-effacing self is displaced. He is now a Mr Hyde — cruel, callous and bent on destruction. But the transition from the self-effacing courteous Malay to the *amok* is always a slow process. It is so slow that it may never come about at all. He may go to his grave before the turmoil in him explodes.

Today the *amok* is only a legend. Civilization has subdued the Malay. He still harbours his resentment, but he is better able to control it. He is a better man for it. But it remains an essential part of his make-up, a basic part of his character.

There are other facets of the Malay character. For the moment they are irrelevant. They are connected with the Malay problem, but they are concerned with the question of solving rather than understanding the potential danger of the problem. They will be discussed later.

This brief examination of certain aspects of the Malay character is merely to illustrate that the Malay problem is more explosive than the evidence seems to indicate. It is meant to focus attention on the peculiarity of the Malays in suppressing their discontent. We can now understand why, throughout history, the Malays appear to be contented to step further and further into the background. They gave up, apparently, politely, almost every vestige of power and authority in their own land.

The British assumed control of the Malay Peninsula imperceptibly, with the seeming cooperation of the Malays, from the sultans down to the humblest villager. The murder of a British Resident hardly interrupted the process, although it made the British devious and artful. They learnt to appreciate the undercurrent of resentment in the Malay, and the conflict between this and his natural courtesy. They learnt how to placate the Malay. They understood just how far they could go. Henceforth, their gradual takeover became marred with no more unpleasant incidents. The immigrant flow, a mere trickle until British rule brought on a deluge, displaced the Malays, seemingly without any opposition from them.

Just before the Second World War there were signs that the Malays were about to break the pernicious bondage that they had imposed on themselves. The *Kesatuan Melayu Muda* was about to come out in open conflict with the British Raj when the Japanese invaded. British Intelligence knew about it, but Westminster did not. Thus the Malayan Union plan was drawn up by a complacent Westminster to finally deprive the Malays of what little authority or position they still had in Malaya. A brash civil servant was assigned the job of giving a semblance of legal authority to what was already an accomplished fact. Once again the undercurrent of resentment threatened to boil over. The Malays who regarded themselves as being merely subjects of their own particular ruler became suddenly united in the face of the danger which threatened them. And once again the British, sensitive and conscious of history, backed down gracefully. The gentleman in the Malay recognized the move. A gentleman had done what a gentleman should. The rapprochement was almost complete. In fact esteem for the British was heightened.

Assured and pacified, the Malay again became the courteous gentleman. But soon it became evident that the British meant to try again. The fight against the principles of the Malayan Union was not over. Cautious and apprehensive after the way they were treated over the Malayan Union affair, the Malays soon enough recognized the more devious methods the British meant to use. On guard, they countered the British moves with the same indirectness. So far, we have seen that the British were adept at handling the

Malays. Every time the situation appeared to get out of hand, the British staged a graceful retreat. The mollified Malays were then confronted with a new and more tactful approach. In the final settlement of accounts, the Malays lost.

While the British remained in Malaya they acted as a buffer between the Malays and the immigrant Chinese and Indians. Contact between these two communities and the Malays was kept to the minimum, both administratively and socially. The presence of the British Protectors of the Chinese, and of the Indian agents, meant that the problems of those immigrant communities were outside the purview of Malay officialdom. Segregation and cultural and language differences prevented social contact. The result was that these immigrants understood little about Malay behaviour and characteristics, and nothing at all about how to handle them.

But Independence removed the British buffer. Suddenly, contact was established at all levels between the Malays and the non-Malays. The situation became gradually more tense as the Malays with their old-fashioned courtesy and unwillingness to embarrass came face to face with people who neither appreciated these qualities nor knew how to handle them. Fortunately, there were sufficient non-Malay leaders at the helm of the Government who knew about the Malay problem and about British methods to avoid the head-on collision that would have occurred. But over the years since Independence the number of enlightened leaders has not been augmented. The newer generation of non-Malay leaders can only see the Malays as an impediment to their communities' desire for unlimited progress. Malay courtesy and fear of anarchy are seen as weaknesses, not to be understood but exploited.

The rift widens. Tolerance gives way to narrow loyalties. The problem grows with each passing day and the conflict within the Malay himself heightens. Courtesy and a desire to avoid unpleasantness battle with the need for self-preservation. How long will good manners and breeding remain dominant? How much can the Malay problem be blown up before it bursts? The answer must lie with the

Malays, the Chinese and the Indians. We have to learn the tactics of the British. We have to learn to understand the problem. We have to know its basis, its proportion and its justification. The cup of Malay bitterness must be diluted. A solution must be found, an equitable solution which denies nothing to anyone and yet gives the Malay his place in the Malayan sun. The Malay problem must be enunciated, analyzed and evaluated so as to enable us to find a solution. The problem must be faced, and it must be faced now before it is too late.

For suddenly, it has dawned upon the Malay that he cannot even call Malaya his land. There is no more *Tanah Melayu* — the Land of the Malays. He is now a different person, a Malaysian, but a Malay Malaysian whose authority in Malaya — his land — is now not only shared with others, but shared unequally. And as if this is not enough, he is being asked to give up more and more of his share of influence.

This is a basic contention of the Malays which is challenged by other races. The Malays maintain that Malaya has always been, and still is, their land. If citizenship must be conferred on other races who have settled down and made their homes in Malaya, it is the Malays who must decide the form of citizenship, the privileges and the obligations. On becoming citizens, the non-Malays share with the Malays not only the ownership of Malaysia, but the specifications of what is a citizen, what is a condition of citizenship itself, and what is therefore not to be changed by the new citizens.

Is Malaya the land of the Malays? After all, the Chinese and even the Indians have been here a long, long time, and have as much claim as the Malays. Besides, the Malays were not the first settlers in Malaya. The aborigines were here before the Malays. If the Malays can take the land from the aborigines, so can the Chinese and Indians. The Chinese and Indians must therefore stand at par with the Malays. This insidious campaign to refute what was once an accepted fact concerning the primary Malay right to Malaya started with the British concept of the Malayan

121

Union. It waxed and waned with the changes in Malayan politics. Finally it culminated in the now famous statement by Mr Lee Kuan Yew, the Prime Minister of Singapore, prior to Singapore's withdrawal from Malaysia, that "We (the Chinese) are here as of right". In other words, the Malays have no greater right to the Malay Peninsula than the Chinese or Indians.

Who owns what country has been a cause of wars and disputes since the beginning of history. Parties to the disputes have never found agreement whatever the merits of the arguments put forth, or the results of battles and wars. It would seem futile to attempt here to give the reasons for the Malay claim. But fortunately there are countries whose problems are similar to Malaya and the acceptance by the world of their citizenship policies and international personality provide us with a basis for bolstering the Malay contention. Australia is one such example. The British who settled in Australia only a few centuries ago were certainly unilaterally appropriating to themselves the land of the Australian aborigines. Yet today no one seriously suggests that the white Australians have less right to govern Australia than the aborigines. The Australians are accepted by international consent as the people of Australia.

International consent and recognition is very important in the establishment of a national identity. This recognition takes many forms. Diplomatic representation is the most concrete form, but where there are no accredited representatives, the government or apparent authority of a land with which foreign nations negotiate, make treaties, and trade, becomes the legal, racial, or national ruler of the territory concerned. The fact that the whole world negotiates and deals with the Australians and not the Australian aborigines establishes the fact that Australia belongs to the immigrant Australians.

We know that the first settlers in Australia were of British extraction. Subsequently there were settlers of other European extraction. But by the time other races came, the Australian was recognizable as an international personality. He was English speaking, practised basically

English customs, and followed the Christian faith. He accepted his link with the British Crown, and even when his country became independent he maintained this link. The establishment of this identity meant that the settlers who came later from other European and even Asian countries had to conform to this identity. Failure to conform would mean failure to obtain legal status as an Australian. The fact that the non-British settler has severed all connections with his original country, and does not intend to leave Australia, does not automatically make him an Australian. It is the definitive Australians who decide when the newcomer can call himself an Australian.

Should he conform to the accepted conditions for becoming an Australian, he obtains legal status and his offspring become Australian. But his rights and those of his offspring as Australians do not extend to insisting that the definition of what is an Australian should be changed so that the language, customs and traditions conform to those of his country of origin. An Australian of Russian origin may not insist that because he has as much right as any other Australians to Australia, the Russian language and customs should become the language and customs of Australia. An Australian Chinese may not ask that the Chinese language and culture be accepted as the language and culture of Australia.

In other words, as the international personality of the Australian has been established, and as the Australians themselves wish to retain this identity, no Australians may try to change it according to their own interpretation. The original English speaking Australians would not tolerate such a move and would take steps to prevent any further weakening of their position by expelling such neo-Australians and stopping the immigration of more like them.

Indeed, the whole immigration, administration, and educational policy is designed to permanently retain the identity of the Australian as a basically white, English speaking person whose customs are British and whose religion is Christianity. Immigration is so controlled that there are always sufficient definitive Australians to dilute the influences of the newcomers.

America is another country with a history and a policy similar to Australia. The Red Indians, though better organized and more advanced than the Australian aborigines, were never regarded internationally as the owners of the United States of America. The people who settled in the various parts of what is now the United States of America were not all of Anglo-Saxon stock, even at the beginning. The thirteen colonies were British. A lot of Dutch people settled in New Amsterdam, later New York. Louisiana in the south was colonized by the French. By sheer weight of numbers and by wars and negotiation, the English speaking Anglo-Saxon stock dominated America and created the definitive image of the Americans. Successive waves of European immigrants, though they eventually outnumbered those of pure British stock, were so regulated that the English language and culture remained the basis of the American identity.

Today in America there are pockets of people who retain the use of the language of their country of origin and some of the customs and religion. The Jews, the Italians, the Puerto Ricans and even the Chinese live in well-defined communities and use their own language. They even have newspapers of their own. They retain links with the "old country". But as Americans they all speak English and do not try to seek recognition of their own language and cultures as the language and culture of the United States. Indeed, the moment they achieve public recognition they try to forget their language and country of origin, try to move out of their ghettoes and set themselves up as average Americans. They then become more American than Americans and they jealously guard the laws of immigration, the educational policy and other paraphernalia of government to preserve the accepted concept of an American.

Nearer home we have Thailand and Vietnam. Thailand has one of the biggest Chinese minority communities. There are, at a rough estimate, some three million Chinese in a

124

country of twenty-five million. In addition a considerable number of Chinese have married Thais and are considered to be Thai. Chinese immigration into Thailand began at about the same time that the Chinese started their adventures into what they still refer to as the southern region. The countries of mainland Southeast Asia were considered as tributary states of Imperial China, and Chinese diplomatic representations were accredited earlier than those of any other country. Eventually the Chinese urge to trade and acquire riches led more and more Chinese to emigrate and settle down in the countries of Southeast Asia. Until recently these Chinese had no wish to claim the citizenship of the countries in which they settled.

In Thailand however the menace of Chinese economic hegemony was early recognized. It is uncertain when the Thais realized that a big unabsorbed Chinese community might make Thailand, already uncomfortably close to China, a tributary state of that Imperial-minded country. But it is certain that very early in the history of Thailand conditions designed to prevent the influence of the growing Chinese community from affecting the national and international identity of the Thais were arbitrarily imposed. Intermarriage and absorption of Thai culture, language and religion were encouraged through restrictions on trade and employment applicable to purely Chinese people. Administration was rigidly retained in Thai hands, or in those of Chinese-Thai extract who conformed to the Thai identity. At no time in the history of Thailand was there any dispute as to who had more right to Thailand. No matter what early foreign communities settled permanently in Thailand, it was the definitive Thai who had the last say as to who should have the right of citizenship. The fact that three million Chinese are now permanent residents of Thailand does not confer on them the right to call themselves Thais and to ask that their language and culture be accepted as the language and the culture of Thailand.

The Chinese were originally in Vietnam as rulers. The Chinese have never been truly absorbed in Vietnam. During French rule the Chinese lived apart from the Vietnamese.

There was never any doubt about the ownership of Vietnam. The Vietnamese inherited Vietnam from the French, and then went on to confine the Chinese (who numbered about two million) in their own communities. The Chinese descendants of conquerors and the Chinese traders who came later are now treated as foreigners, with no rights of citizenship. The Chinese must have been longer in Vietnam than anywhere else in Southeast Asia. Their countries are contiguous, their religion similar and their names often hardly distinguishable. But the Vietnamese insist that they and they alone own Vietnam and they decide who and what is Vietnamese.

There are other areas in Southeast Asia where the Chinese have been for as long as they have been in Malaya. But nowhere have they claimed to be or have they been accepted as indigenous peoples of these areas.

The burden of my argument is that the Malays are the rightful owners of Malaya, and that if citizenship is conferred on races other than the Malays, it is because the Malays consent to this. That consent is conditional.

The first conclusion from the study of other countries is that the presence of aborigines prior to settlement by other races does not mean that the country is internationally recognized as belonging to the aborigines. Aborigines are found in Australia, Taiwan and Japan, to name a few, but nowhere are they regarded as the definitive people of the country concerned. The definitive people are those who set up the first governments and these governments were the ones with which other countries did official business and had diplomatic relations.

There is another condition. The people who form the first effective Government and their legal successors must at all times outnumber the original tribes found in a given country. This is so in the countries I have mentioned, but in South Africa, Kenya and Rhodesia the original people outnumber the races who formed the first effective governments.

We know the attitude of the modern world to the situation in these countries. Although the white government of Kenya

126

was the first effective government, modern opinion insists that the original black Africans, because they outnumber the whites and because they were the original people of the area, should be the government and the definitive people of Kenya. In time, pressure of world opinion forced this change in Kenya. The same argument applies in South Africa and Rhodesia. Despite the fact that the white settlers in these two countries formed the first effective Governments, and have been internationally accepted for a long time as the definitive people, they are still being asked to make way for the black Africans who grossly outnumber them and who are ethnically associated with the regions.

In Malaya, the Malays without doubt formed the first effective governments. The Malay states have been internationally recognized since the beginning of Malayan history. Trade, treaties and diplomatic representation by foreign countries were negotiated with the Malay-governed Malay states of Malaya. The *Orang Melayu* or Malays have always been the definitive people of the Malay Peninsula. The aborigines were never accorded any such recognition nor did they claim such recognition. There was no known aborigine government or aborigine state. Above all, at no time did they outnumber the Malays. It is quite obvious that if today there were four million aborigines, the right of the Malays to regard the Malay Peninsula as their own country would be questioned by the world. But in fact there are no more than a few thousand aborigines.

Imperial China exacted tributes from some of the Malay states. This in itself was a form of Chinese recognition of the existence of the Malay states and of the legality of the Malay governments. It can be seen, therefore, that if international practice be any indication, the Malays are truly the definitive people of the Malay Peninsula, the real and original rulers and owners of Malaya. No other race has any grounds to dispute this. History, especially recent history, bolsters the Malay contention. All dealings by foreign governments and people were with Malay rajas as the rulers of the country. No one else ever arrogated to himself the right to enter into any agreement or treaty on behalf of the peninsula. Malacca was won by the Portuguese from the Malays. Subsequently, the Portuguese lost this territory to the Dutch, and the Dutch to the British. Penang was leased to the British by the Malay Sultan of Kedah. Later, Province Wellesley was added to the territory of British Penang also by agreement with the Sultan of Kedah. The Dindings and Pangkor were leased by the Malay Sultan of Perak. When these two territories were no longer useful to the British they were returned to the ruler of Perak. No questions were asked as to whether the colonial subjects of the British in these two territories should be the successors of the British. They were never even consulted. And no protests or agitation followed the return of the Dindings and Pangkor to Perak.

In the case of Singapore, the British cheated the Maharaja of Johore. It is quite obvious that but for the secret switch of rulers in Johore engineered by the British, Singapore would not have been ceded to the British. That it was necessary to do all these things shows that the British recognized Malay rights over the island of Singapore.

In the subsequent history of the British administration of Malaya, the Malays and the Malay rulers were the only people consulted and recognized by the British as the definitive people of Malaya. In the Straits Settlements the British ruled without reference to the Malays. This was possible because the Malay rulers were in no position to protest. The Sultan of Kedah did attempt to regain Penang, but met with ignominious defeat at the hands of British mercenaries. Following this affair it was thought best to leave the British alone. It was obvious to the Malays that when territories were leased to the British, the British behaved not as lessees, but as outright owners or landlords. Unless the force necessary to defeat the British physically was available, any attempt to make the British revise their interpretation of the word lease would be futile.

Elsewhere in the Malay Peninsula the British ruled through the Malays. Admittedly the Malays had no choice but to obey the British. The hypocrisy of the words written into the various treaties with the British by which the

Malay rulers "must accept the advice of the British Advisers when advice was offered", would have shamed any other people except the British. This device enabled the British to do just what they liked. And what they liked knew no limit. It included the removal of sultans and tampering with the laws of succession.

But the fact remains that the British ruled Malaya through the Malays and not through anyone else. It is true that advisory legislative bodies included a few non-Malays. But the function of these bodies was so far removed from the executive that it can be said that their existence was merely to assuage British conscience. The non-Malays were never true legislators but were merely rubber-stamps. All major changes such as the creation of the Federated Malay States and the proposed Customs Union, which was to include all the states of Malaya, were negotiated directly with the sultans as the true executive heads of each state.

The conquest of Malaya by the Japanese did not alter the position of the Malay rulers. The Japanese left them as sultans, although the Japanese Military Government did not feel the need to consult them on matters of administration or policy. Halfway through the war in Southeast Asia the four northern Malay states were transferred by the Japanese to Thailand. The Thais ruled through military governors but they likewise did not abolish the sultanates. Indeed, the sultans were in a more privileged position than they were under the Japanese.

The defeat of Japan was followed by many changes in the administration of territories formerly under British protection. Rajah Brooke of Sarawak and the British North Borneo Company were asked to surrender their authority in these two territories to the British Government. They had no choice. When one of the Brookes protested, the measures taken against him were indicative of British determination. Even the killing of a British Governor of Sarawak did not deter the British.

For Malaya, the British plan ignored for the first time their previous practice of consultation with the Malay rulers of the country. The then Labour Government of Britain, with little or no knowledge of the country, felt that the Malay sultans were not democratic enough. Their status was therefore to be reduced to that of chief priests, and the administration of the country taken over completely by the British. In addition, all who lived in Malaya would become citizens and have the same rights as the Malays. This was in keeping with the generous mood of the British where property belonging to others was concerned. In Palestine for example the whole country was taken from the Arabs and handed over to the Jews.

The British sense of formality nevertheless still persisted. Although they had the authority and the force to ignore the sultans and the Malays, they insisted on getting formal consent from the sultans for the proposed Malayan Union. Fittingly an officer from Palestine was chosen to do this. With unseemly haste the consent was extracted from the nine Malay rulers after a threat of non-recognition should there be any intransigence. The point to be made here is that even at that most critical period in the relationship between the Malays and the British, the British still formally recognized the legal authority of the Malay sultans in the states of the Malay Peninsula. This was emphasized when serious agitation and unrest among the Malays later forced the British to abandon their plans for a Malayan Union and restore the status of the Malay rulers.

Henceforth all changes leading up to the Independence of Malaya in 1957 were made in full consultation and agreement not only with the Malay rulers but also with the Malay people as represented by the major Malay political party, the United Malays National Organization. It is plain therefore that until the surrender of their authority on Merdeka Day in August 1957, the British recognized the Malays as the only people whose consent must be obtained before any changes could be made in Malaya. The other communities were also consulted but no proposal objectionable to the Malays had a chance of getting through.

Since Independence there have been other arguments about the Chinese and Indians having as much right as the Malays to claim Malaya as their own country. These claims ignore all precedents and facts of history. One of the more interesting claims is that the Chinese and Indians are the people who have developed Malaya and made it prosperous. This seems to confer on developers the right of ownership without regard to other considerations.

In the first place this statement is not quite true. A variety of factors have contributed to the development of Malaya, and all communities have contributed towards this. Malay tolerance of mass immigration cannot be considered an unimportant factor. If the Malays had objected at first, there would have been no immigrants to develop Malaya. Not only have the Malays allowed immigration, they were also responsible for ruling and policing the country so that wealth could be accumulated by immigrants without fear of expropriation. It is true that in this work they were advised and assisted by the British, but this merely goes to show that the British are also responsible for developing the country and making it prosperous. In the second place the immigrants did not come to Malaya to develop it. They came because of the wealth to be gained in an atmosphere of tolerance and stability which differentiated Malaya from all the other Southeast Asian colonies and countries. The benefits of this development accrue mainly to the wealth-seeking immigrants. The Malays who lived mostly in rural areas did not get much benefit from these developments and prosperity. If there had been no developments they would not have cared very much either. They would certainly not give up their claims to Malaya for the prosperity they could not share.

The question this claim raises is whether people who develop a country are automatically entitled to it. If mere development entitles any race of settlers to the country in which they settled, then surely the British would have first claim in Malaya, Kenya and other colonial territories. The Chinese have also contributed largely to the development of the Philippines, Thailand, Indonesia and Vietnam. But until these Chinese settler-developers fulfil a complicated series of conditions, which may include changing their names and marrying definitive citizens, they may not claim these countries as their own. In the United States, immigrants who are selected for their ability to contribute to the development of the country, have still to fulfil a variety of residential qualifications, including language tests, before they can become citizens and so claim the United States as their own country.

Nowhere is the mere fact of contribution to the development and prosperity of a country the sole criterion for claiming that the contributor owns the country. Therefore, the claim that the Chinese and Indians are responsible for the development of Malaya still does not confer on these immigrants and their descendents the same status as the indigenous Malays. They must satisfy a series of conditions before they can achieve this.

Yet another argument is that innumerable immigrants have lived in Malaya for one generation and more, and have severed relations with their own countries of origin. These people claim that as their loyalty is only to Malaya, they must have Malayan citizenship and be equal to the Malays. It is easy to claim loyalty. To prove loyalty, certain conditions of stress must arise. Even then it is not possible to prove all the claims. Immigrants may say that Malaya is their only country. They were born in Malaya, they have worked here and they have property here. They will die here and be buried here. Like the Malays, they have no other country to go to or to call home. At home and abroad they are Malayans.

But the fact remains that should a Malay and an Indian be forced to leave Malaya, the Indian can settle down in India and be an Indian whilst the Malay cannot. Similarly the Chinese, whatever he himself may think, is still acceptable to China should he find the need to go back. Indeed, we have no knowledge of Indians from Malaya being refused citizenship of India should they seek Indian citizenship. Similarly, overseas Chinese from Indonesia and Malaya were accepted with open arms by China when they were ejected for political reasons. Where can the Malays go if they should be banished from Malaya? They would find no country which would accept them as a national because of racial ties. Even Indonesia does not regard the Malays as originally from Indonesia and will not automatically accept Malay exiles.

To be truly indigenous one must belong to no other race but that truly identified with a given country. If one's racial origin is identifiable and acceptable to any other country, one is no longer indigenous and cannot claim the country one has settled in as one's own. This is not to say that if all the other qualifications of citizenship are fulfilled this claim cannot be valid. But mere claim of loyalty or belonging does not in itself justify citizenship.

We are now in the process of building a new nation which is to be an amalgam of different racial groups. The form of this new nation and new citizenship must be such as to satisfy all the constituent races. An understanding of the relative rights and claims of each race is important if we are to avoid the differences which selfish racial prejudices will engender. This understanding must be universal and widespread. And above all, the understanding must be based on reasoned arguments and not mere sentiments and selfish motivations.

I contend that the Malays are the original or indigenous people of Malaya and the only people who can claim Malaya as their one and only country. In accordance with practice all over the world, this confers on the Malays certain inalienable rights over the forms and obligations of citizenship which can be imposed on citizens of non-indigenous origin. Before discussing what these rights are and how far the Malays have claimed or insisted on them, it is worth noting that in Malaya even the limited exercise of these rights has been more obvious than it should be. The reason is quite easy to see. The conferment of citizenship on non-Malay communities which are heterogeneous, unassimilated and too large to be manageable was made rather hastily. In other countries of Southeast Asia (and in Australia, America and Brazil), the process of extending citizenship was gradual and controlled by far-sighted immigration policies. As small groups of immigrants of different racial origin acquired citizenship, they adopt the characteristics and distinctive language and culture of the larger definitive race of the country concerned. Forgetting their ancestry, these new citizens not only become indistinguishable from the definitive race but they in turn insist on retaining the conditions of citizenship to which they had to submit. The process of retaining and perpetuating the identity of the definitive race which at first was artificially devised becomes, as it were, self-priming and acquires a momentum of its own. It takes advantage of certain human values and traits. The perpetual position of being in the minority and underprivileged creates a desire in the new immigrants to merge with the majority and acquire the privileged position. The immediate loss of original culture, language and racial characteristics is insignificant when compared with the privileges to be gained as citizens. And having gained these privileges and been accepted as equals, natural human jealousy takes over and guards the conditions of their status. This process once started can only be thrown out of gear when there is a massive influx of aggressive and sophisticated immigrants of a particular racial group.

In Malaysia there is evidence that but for British rule this was what would have happened. The Chinese and Indians who came to Malaya before the British extended their influence, showed some evidence of undergoing a typical process of assimilation. In Malacca the Chinese and Indians lost the use of their own languages and adopted the Malay language. They also adopted Malay dress and Malay culture although they retained their own religion. It is certain that had the British not encouraged the Chinese and Indians to immigrate in unmanageable numbers and then segregated them from the Malays, these people would have fewer differences with the Malays, and the Malay problem would not have emerged. As it is, the imposition of even the minimal conditions of citizenship on large heterogeneous groups accustomed to certain rights without obligations have attracted undue attention.

To return to the question of the rights of the original people, we can say that these too are limited. The aim of these rights and the exercise of them are not designed to perpetuate the privileges of the original definitive race to the exclusion of the newer immigrant races, but only to ensure the perpetuation of the characteristics of the definitive race. The ethnic origin is therefore unimportant, and does not disqualify the newer settlers. All that this imposition of conditions means is that settlers willing to conform to the characteristics of the definitive citizen will in fact become definitive citizens and will exercise the same rights and privileges. But these rights and privileges do not include changing the characteristics of the definitive race. This emphasis on definitive characteristics rather than ethnic origin is an important principle and its application is also seen in the limitation of the rights of newer citizens to change these characteristics.

In Malaya the Malays always· recognized this principle and the acceptance of non-Malays who acquire Malay characteristics has gone on throughout the history of the country. The only extra limitation is the insistence that a Malay, by definition, is one who professes the Islamic faith. This insistence has confined the acquisition of Malay citizenship to Indonesians, Arabs and Indian Muslims. Thus we have Malays who are distinctly Arab, Indonesian or Indian. The important thing is that these people not only conform to all the Malay characteristics but insist on the criteria for becoming Malays being perpetuated.

In other countries, the rights of the citizens of immigrant origins concerning the control and perpetuation of their own distinctive characteristics are limited. This limitations varies with different countries. On the other hand the control of measures to perpetuate the distinctive national characteristics of a country is the concern not only of the original definitive citizens but also of the citizens by naturalization. It is the duty of all citizens to submit to and to insist upon those policies with regard to language, immigration, culture etc. which are calculated to create and preserve the distinctive national characteristics.

Language is admittedly the most important characteristic. The language of the nationals of any country normally distinguishes them from others. The exception is the English language, which has, by an accident of history, become the national language of countries other than England. The principle nevertheless applies: —that the perpetuation of the language originally adopted as the national language, becomes the right and the concern of the original as well as the naturalized people. In Malaya, Malay is the language of the original people who set up the first effective government. It is therefore logical that Malay should be the national language. The Malay language may undergo various changes through the incorporation of new words and new constructions but it must at all times be recognizable as the Malay language.

It may be argued that as Malay is also basically the language of Indonesia, it is no more indigenous to Malaya than Chinese or Indian. But the Indonesian language is not indigenous to Indonesia. In the islands of Indonesia a wide variety of languages distinctly related to Malay are spoken. Thus in Java, Javanese is mainly spoken, while in Sumatra there are the Achinese, the Mendahiling, the Minangkabau and other Sumatran languages. In the Celebes another language, which also bears some vague similarity to Malay, is spoken. By an accident of history, Malay, the language of Malacca and the rest of the Malay Peninsula, Riau as well as a small part of Sumatra, became the lingua franca of the whole Malay archipelago. When the first political awakenings stirred the different peoples of what is now Indonesia, this lingua franca was the only means of communication and was extensively used as a unifying factor. It is natural that it was later adopted as the national language of Indonesia. But the people in the different parts of Indonesia still use their own dialects when in their own closed communities. It is only in the states of the Malay Peninsula that Malay is the common language of the indigenous people. Malay is truly the indigenous language of Malaya. As the language of the first people to settle and form effective governments in the peninsula, it has priority over other languages as the definitive language of the country.

There are other reasons for accepting Malay. But they are not relevant to the present discussion which concerns the right of the original people to perpetuate this aspect of their character. Their language distinguishes them from other nationals, and, when adopted by new non-Malay citizens, would similarly distinguish them.

In this matter of national language the rights of new citizens are limited. They may not seek to replace it with other languages, even though technically and legally this can be done. The national language of Malaya is clearly stated in the Constitution. As the Constitution may be changed on the agreement of two-thirds of the Members of Parliament, it would seem that a change in the national language could possibly be moved by new citizens. Any such move however would be against the spirit with which citizenship was offered by the Malays, and accepted by non-Malays.

The fact that in Malaya the number of non-Malay speaking citizens is disproportionately high might be used as a reason for departing from the practice usual elsewhere. Nevertheless, it is important to remember that the increase in the number of non-Malay speaking citizens is by consent of the Malays on the tacit understanding that the criteria of citizenship should not only be followed but should remain unalterable. It is certain that Malay agreement to the liberal granting of citizenship to residents of non-Malay origin would not have been forthcoming had there been any suspicion that the new citizens intended to change the language in any way. The common practice in other parts of the world reassured the Malays that a non-Malay citizen could not change the basic position of the Malay language as the distinctive language of the people of Malaya.

But the Malays with their usual tolerance have not insisted on true exclusiveness for the national language which in other countries is taken as a matter of course. The continued usage and growth of other immigrant languages is not only permitted but is actually guaranteed in the Constitution. The harsh suppression of immigrant languages common in other Southeast Asian countries, and the more

137

effective but less obvious control in Australia and America are not insisted on in Malaya. The qualifying language tests for intending citizens are negligible compared to those in Australia and America. Indeed, it can be said that the Malays have actually helped in the propagation of non-Malay languages by acceding to demands for Government-aided non-Malay schools for the exclusive use of non-Malay citizens.

All these things tend to smother the use and growth of the Malay language as the definitive language. And such is the desire of the Malays not to be unpleasant and a source of embarrassment, that they have led themselves into a dilemma which would be unthinkable elsewhere.

Today there is an attempt on the part of the new citizens to go completely against precedence and practice. The demand for the use of immigrant languages has become more strident, more unreasonable. In the colonial days, the use of English in all government documents was taken for granted. Those who could not understand English were expected to find their own interpreters. Signs and notices, with few exceptions, were in English, and if at times these signs were only useful to a handful of people, this was expected and tolerated. Malay, even in the colonial days was used more frequently and better understood than English. It is even more so now. Yet the exclusive use of Malay, the national language, in documents and notices is resisted on the grounds that few of the older non-Malay citizens can understand it. But no protest was made in the past when these same people could not understand English.

The use of non-Malay immigrant languages has actually increased over Radio Malaysia. Lack of knowledge of Chinese dialects is even a bar to employment in some public companies. The University of Malaya does research into and teaches Chinese and Tamil. Chinese is taught at English medium schools, and if there is a demand, may be taught in Malay medium schools. Cinemas carry Chinese subtitles for Western pictures but no sub-titles in the national language. Increased employment of non-Malay speaking officers in public service means that Malays going to these officers cannot speak directly to them, but have to use interpreters.

All this cannot happen in any of the countries around Malaysia. Nor in Australia or America. But in Malaysia non-Malay citizens are actually insisting that not enough is being done to promote and extend the use of these foreign languages. The Government is being urged to widen governmental use of Chinese and to sponsor Chinese education from the lowest level up to university level. Exclusively Chinese educational qualifications are accepted as adequate for employment in the public services. Through all this the Malays remained passive. Courteous and gentle as ever, the majority raised no objections. The leaders urged calmness and some actually advocated even more tolerance. Confused and paralyzed, the Malays endure the difficulty in which they find themselves over the language question, not with a sense of righteousness but with the fatality of people of the Islamic faith. And the signs are that this will remain the Malay attitude. Any appreciation of the Malay language problem and any act in fairness to the Malays must therefore come from the non-Malays, the more sophisticated among whom realize the justice of the Malay claim.

The control of immigration is normally one of the methods by which the people of any country maintain their characteristics. This is particularly so in countries founded through settling and colonizing by racial groups from other countries, as in the case of Australia, New Zealand, America and the Latin American countries. Had the Malays of the Malay Peninsula controlled immigration in the past they would have ensured that at no time would they, as the definitive people of the country, be threatened with extinction. But the Malays failed to do this. Not because they did not realize the dangers, but because of a combination of tolerance and *laissez faire* attitude, and their trust in others.

Prior to the coming of the Portuguese, there was a scattering of foreign traders of Arab, Indian and Chinese origin who had more or less settled in the various parts of the Malay states. These people, cut off from their

139

homeland, tended to absorb Malay characteristics and be absorbed by the Malays. The most resistant group was the Chinese who, although they adopted the language, the dress and even the social activities of the Malays, remained distinct and unintegrated. Nevertheless, for as long as the reins of Government were in the hands of the Malays, the unabsorbable immigrants could not sufficiently increase in number to challenge the Malays.

In any case, excessive immigration did not take place until Malacca, and later Penang and Singapore, were lost by the Malays. Complete foreign control of these city ports excluded the Malays from any say on immigration. They were in no position to act upon any fear they might have entertained over the increased influx of Chinese and Indians. The result was that these colonies became staging posts for Chinese and Indian invasion of the hinterland. They did not come as settlers at first but as merchants and traders. The scruples of the Malay rajas and chiefs were overcome through lavish gifts and direct profit sharing which has always been a feature of Chinese business. Opium and gambling monopolies granted to Chinese merchants yielded rich returns to the Malay chiefs. And they found too that more could be made from turning over mining to the Chinese than from mining themselves.

The qualms the rulers might have felt about the increased number of Chinese and Indians in the country were stilled by the rich harvest from various levies imposed on the immigrants' enterprises. In those days the immigrants gave no indication that they wished to settle and claim citizenship rights, much less did they show that they even wanted the character of the nationals of the Malay states changed to conform with their own specifications. They were for the most part Chinese and Indian nationals, out to make their fortune and then return to their own country. If they had houses in Malaya, these were mainly in the British colonies of Penang, Malacca and Singapore, which they used as their bases of operation. Thus, when the British extended their rule into the Malay states, the non-Malay immigrant communities were already present in some numbers. The British, whose appreciation of Chinese and Indian usefulness has already been pointed out, set about encouraging increased immigration almost as soon as they had effective rule of the country. For them there was everything to be gained. As far as they could see, any losses would accrue to the Malays.

After some time the Malays were sufficiently alarmed to act. But, because by then the British were the *de facto* rulers of the country, the only action that the awakened Malays could take was one of passive resistance. They did not ask for control of immigration, but rather voiced their fears of being disregarded as the real nationals of the country. The British were equal to the situation. They suggested various measures to safeguard the Malays which they explained would be sufficient to ensure that the Malay Peninsula remained a Malay country. These safeguards for the Malays and their sultans, centered round an exclusively Malay Civil Service and reservations of land for Malays only. Later they were circumvented by the British and the non-Malays; but these measures, once they were suggested, again lulled the Malays into a false sense of security. The fear they were beginning to feel over the greatly increased Chinese and Indian immigration was stilled for a time, and the move to close the floodgates was put off.

But by the beginning of the Second World War, Malay apprehension was once more aroused. The Japanese conquest of Malaya crushed Malay faith in the British ability to protect them. When the British returned and proposed the Malayan Union with its policy of equal citizenship for all, this loss of faith in British ability was reinforced by loss of faith in British integrity. The fear of immigrant domination became a reality even for the Malay rulers. During the subsequent protests against the Malayan Union, control of immigration became a matter of urgency for Malay nationalists. Since the granting of full citizenship rights to immigrants was no longer the ridiculous thing the Malays thought it was before the war, a situation where the immigrants might outnumber the indigenous people could never be allowed. Indeed, in the days when the Malays looked to Indonesia for inspiration, there were serious schemes to encourage the immigration of the easily assimilable Indonesians in order to retain and even increase Malay numerical superiority.

It would have seemed logical that the moment the Malays regained control of the destiny of their country from the British they would rush to regulate immigration to their own advantage. Although the Government which succeeded the British was a coalition of Malays, Chinese and Indians, the Malays were still strong enough to do this. But once again the Malay sense of courtesy and fair play intervened. The Malay-dominated Government compromised, and did not insist on positive steps to use an immigration policy to build up their own racial strength. They were content to leave matters alone and to leave the actual implementation of the immigration policy in the hands of non-Malays. Indeed, they closed their eyes to known instances where non-Malay immigrants had slipped into the country because the immigration laws were not strictly adhered to. They did this because they did not like to embarrass non-Malay friends and colleagues who were invariably behind these breaches of good faith. This became another problem. With the means to better their political strength in their own hands, the Malays let the opportunity slip by because they did not have the heart to do what others have done. Control of immigration in other countries has always been a means to retain political control in the hands of the definitive race. The definitive people of Malaya failed to do this. And this happened by choice. Natural courtesy once again got the better of the Malays. All this would be worthwhile if it was appreciated. But the evidence is that it is not only not appreciated, but these acts are in fact looked on as a sign of weakness and the result of a lack of conviction among the Malays themselves as to their special rights as the definitive original people of Malaya.

The education policy of any country, apart from its function of imparting and promoting knowledge, is invariably a means of instilling into the minds of future citizens a

sense of oneness, loyalty and pride in the country. In relatively new countries considerable use is made of education.
In America and Australia the definitive races use education
to implant in the minds of future citizens who have different
antecedents that, as citizens of these countries, they automatically belong to and inherit the culture and characteristics of the definitive people. Thus the German-American
is made to see more significance in the spirit of '76 than
in the glories of the German Empire. And the Greek Australian knows more of Botany Bay than of Greece's past
glory.

The language medium is of extreme importance in creating a feeling of oneness, and so the medium of instruction
is always that of the definitive race. It occurs to no one to
demand that the language of the new immigrants should be
the medium of instruction. But language is not the only
important aspect of a national education policy. The whole
curriculum is important. The teaching of history, geography, and literature are all designed to propagate one
idea; that the country belongs to the definitive people, and
to belong to the country, and to claim it, entails identification with the definitive people. This identification is all-
pervading and leaves no room for identification with other
countries and cultures. To be identified with the definitive
people is to accept their history, their geography, their
literature, their language and their culture, and to reject
anything else.

The educational system is always single and national.
With the exception of Canada there is no country which provides for the education of immigrant races in the language
of the immigrants. Even Canada is not truly representative
of this practice, for the French were not immigrants into an
English-based nation. They were there before the British.

In Southeast Asian countries other than in Malaysia,
these principles are clearly adhered to in formulating national education policies. The definitive people, the people
who formed the first effective government invariably shape
the education policy so that the citizens of the future will
preserve and propagate the language, the culture and

sometimes the religion which distinguishes them. This is the practice and this is the privilege and right of the definitive people. The immigrants are not barred. They are accepted, but they are accepted on the terms of the definitive people. And one of the terms is that the education policy must be that of the definitive people.

This basic principle has been ignored in Malaya. The British are responsible. Disregarding what they had done for their own race in the colonies in which they settled, such as Australia and New Zealand, they permitted the development of education in Malaya to be extra-national. Almost any type of school was allowed, every language medium was used, every curriculum permitted. Nothing seemed unusual. There were Malay schools whose only purpose was to increase literacy and whose curricula carried not even a hint of a national or even regional orientated education policy. There were English schools for the production of semi-educated white-collar workers more loyal to the British Imperial system and the myth of the mother country than to their own country of domicile. There were Tamil schools which were completely purpose-less. There were missionary schools dedicated to education and the spread of the Christian faith. There were Arabic schools, outside the control of the British, but which nevertheless flourished. And finally there were the Chinese schools which were nothing more than little Chinas transplanted into Malaya. The whole system of Chinese education during the British regime was nothing more than an extension of the Chinese national education system which was formulated in the nineteenth and early twentieth centuries, and pursued with extreme vigour.

The oddity of the whole education set-up was never mentioned by the people responsible for advising the Malay governments. Indeed there is evidence that the idea of a national education system was purposely suppressed. While all the other independent countries including the new British Dominions and the United States were already employing education to build up national identification and loyalties, Malaya was kept ignorant of these developments. Acquisition

144

of literacy was treated as an end in itself and not a means to other, greater things. It followed that education and national identification were two different things, and therefore a foreign education system such as Chinese education was not out of place.

The acceptance of this abnormal situation as completely normal set the basis of the difficulties which now beset the Malaysian national education programme. Used to doing just what they liked, the Chinese and Indians can only see injustice in the imposition of an education system which tends to eliminate their foreign orientated schools. They can see nothing wrong in a nation propagating and encouraging the languages, cultures and systems of other nations. And they refuse to accept the precedents and practice of other countries in the field of education.

Faced with this situation the Malays have not invoked their rights as the definitive people of the country. This would embarrass their colleagues and friends in the other communities. Generously, the Malays have offered to compromise. This generosity is not acknowledged. It is taken as a matter of course. The concessions the Malays made are many and varied, and began with their abandonment of the Arabic-based script which they had evolved as their national script. On the surface this seems trivial, but if it is compared to the resentment that the Malayan Chinese would evince at any abandonment of Chinese characters, the sacrifice can be considered to be of some magnitude. If we remember that the Malays still have to burden themselves with this script for the sake of their religion, the concession is indeed remarkable. But this is not their only concession. The language and systems of other nations are allowed to remain a part of the pseudo-national Malaysian education system.

These languages and education systems are separated from the Malay-based education system not merely by language and curricula differences, but also physically, by being housed in separate buildings and locations, with separate teachers and administrations and an employment system limited by racial origins. In some instances these

145

foreign education systems reach higher levels than the Malay-based education. Still the demand for concessions goes on, and will go on for as long as the Malays refuse to embarrass others by insisting that, as the definitive people, they have the right to design the form of national education.

The abnormal educational practice of the British regime must be recognized for what it was. Once this is acknowledged, the implementation of a truly Malaysian national education system will meet with less harassment from people who openly demand the unusual as a matter of right. The Malays must face this problem firmly and not with an air of trepidation resulting from lack of confidence in their rights. In the long run, a truly Malaysian national education system must be recognized and accepted by all citizens as the only means of moulding a single, united nation. Once this policy is accepted and set in motion, it will develop its own momentum. No longer will the Malays have to insist on it, but all who become citizens of Malaysia, irrespective of racial origins and culture, will uphold and impose this educational policy.

In the days when mass emigration was unknown and communication was poor, citizenship was no problem in most countries. Dispersed small groups of immigrants with no access to their countries of origin tended to be rapidly assimilated. Once this happened, the natural antagonism and jealousy directed at foreigners with different cultures disappeared, and citizenship was conferred and accepted as a matter of course. In fact there was no talk of legal citizenship as such, for identification with the definitive people was so complete as to defy questioning.

In England for example, a fair number of French people immigrated at the time of the Norman conquerors. Over the years these people lost most of their French characteristics and became English in their speech, behaviour and sentiments. The difficulty in communication prevented them from keeping up with contemporary French culture. Gradually, without the need for a legal conferment of citizenship, they became English. No conscious effort was involved.

146

In the Malay Peninsula this same process was common prior to the coming of the British. Immigrant traders of Arab, Indian and Chinese origin absorbed Malay culture, including language and dress, and were well on the way to becoming Malay citizens if the balanced immigration and assimilation had not been upset. But the deluge of immigrants which the British encouraged, and the segregation which followed, arrested this healthy, natural process and precipitated the problems which have plagued the Malays ever since, and which have undermined their rights as the definitive people of the peninsula.

It is this massive immigration and the improved communication between the immigrants and their countries of origin which make citizenship a matter of concern to the definitive people, and the control of citizenship their special right. All over the world it is an accepted principle that citizenship of a country is controlled to suit the definitive people. To this end immigration is controlled. But more important, the choice of immigrants who may acquire citizenship is also the rightful responsibility of the definitive people. Laws and regulations for the acquisition of citizenship in most countries are therefore so couched as to prevent immigrants from reversing the position and forcing the definitive people to acquire their characteristics. In other words, the laws are designed to prevent conquest, for when immigrants retain their own cultures and also assume political and economic control of a country, they would in fact have conquered the original people. It is irrelevant to argue that these immigrants are prepared to defend the country to the last drop of their blood; they would merely be defending the country they conquered.

Citizenship is never regarded as an immigrant's right. Citizenship is usually a form of recognition and can only be conferred when the original people feel that an immigrant has demonstrated loyalty, and has truly identified himself with the definitive people. Where people of similar ethnic groups are concerned, even though the original language and culture may be different, this recognition is usually easy to come by. Where different ethnic groups

147

are involved, even after they have acquired the language, culture and characteristics of a definitive people, recognition still presents difficulties. In many Southeast Asian countries, although immigrants have become almost indistinguishable from indigenous people, citizenship has not been automatically conferred. In European countries, Asians and Africans who have almost lost contact with their own cultures, and who have acquired those of the countries in which they settled, have also found difficulty in obtaining citizenship. A variety of arbitrary barriers are placed in their way. It is only after some exceptional achievement that recognition of real equality comes. This is illustrated by the Japanese-Americans who only became acceptable as Americans after their tremendous sacrifices during the Second World War.

As citizenship is a form of recognition, immigrants all over the world are found to be particular about copying and displaying the distinctive characteristics of the definitive people. In America and Australia it is usual for immigrants to be more American or Australian than the definitive Americans and Australians. The same is true of accepted immigrants in Southeast Asian countries. Indeed, immigrant citizens in Southeast Asian countries often appear harsher than original citizens towards new immigrants. New citizens feel that unless complete identification is emphasized they are suspect, and therefore they tend to want to prove their absolute rejection of their foreign origin.

The Japanese-Americans who fought so well for America during the Pacific war were doing just this. In peace such opportunities do not present themselves. It is therefore in everyday life that the immigrants try to prove the sincerity of their identification. Most Chinese immigrants now settled in America not only try to forget their own four thousand year old language and culture, but they are actually proud of having done so. Chinese Filipinos are on record as saying that discrimination against foreign Chinese is actually a good thing. Chinese Thais use the Thai language exclusively in their own home. Chinese Indonesians demonstrate against China. Names are changed so that they sound like those of the definitive people. Religion may be discarded in favour of the common religion of the country of adoption.

Except where ethnic origin is extremely obvious, the process of identification is usually completed within two or three generations. Once this is achieved, sentiments, reactions and behaviour would automatically reflect an identification with the country and the definitive people. The offspring of immigrants would be so identified with the people of the country that they would regard themselves as the definitive people.

In Malaysia, before the coming of the British, the few immigrants were either already absorbed or were on the way to being absorbed. The British era saw a vastly increased influx of immigrants, firstly into the colonies of the Straits Settlements, and then the Malay states. The question of citizenship did not arise, except in the Straits Settlements where a form of citizenship was rather indiscriminately accorded to immigrants. In the rest of the Malay Peninsula the Malays were legally the only citizens and the accepted definitive people. Even when immigration increased there was no thought of conferring citizenship rights on the more permanent of these newcomers. Right up to the end of the Second World War the Malays only had an immigration problem. Citizenship was regarded as the exclusive right and concern of the Malays and the Malays alone and was not regarded as a problem.

It is now clear that even though the immigrants were not interested in being permanent citizens, and did not actually agitate for this status, they had long resented the barrier which citizens presented against their unlimited acquisitiveness and expansion of their sphere of activities. While still wanting to retain their status as citizens of foreign countries, they could not see the citizens' justification for this barrier. They not only wanted parity in treatment by the various state governments and the Imperial power, but they also desired changes to be made in their favour in the structure and administration of Malaya. The lack of a centralized Government machinery together with custom barriers between the states made trading difficult, and this was much disliked by Chinese immigrant traders. The limited administrative authority of the Malay citizens was also a source of irritation, and they could not understand the failure of the British to treat the Malay states as they treated the Straits Settlements.

Even in the 1920's, when immigrant Chinese business-men favoured moves to centralize the governments of the Malay states and to create a common custom area (with the resultant curtailment of the authority of the Malay sul-tan), it occurred to no one to suggest the creation of a Malay nationality as a means of reconciling immigrant aspira-tions with the privileged position of the Malays as definitive citizens. If all the policies on immigration, education and citizenship now in force in Malaysia were imposed then, the resulting smaller number of immigrants, coupled with the relatively poor communication with their own countries would have obviated the citizenship problems which face the Malays today. But the British valued Chinese enterprise and Indian labour too much to think of the fate of the Malays. There were the so-called safeguards in administration and land, and the Malays were reassured of their efficacy and the permanence of their status as the only rightful citizens of Malaya. In the meantime, a half-hearted attempt was made to control immigration. No attempt was made to im-press on an immigrant that as an immigrant and an alien, he must accept certain limitations in line with practice all over the world.

With the failure to fully centralize the governments of the Malay states, and the continued safeguarding of Malay rights, there was no thought of extending citizenship until the Malayan Union was proposed by the British after the War. Suddenly the Malays were confronted with the ugly fact that British adherence to agreed policies could be uni-laterally broken by the British. The proposal to give equal citizenship rights to all residents of Malaya was so shock-ing that even the apathy of the Malays over the lowering of their status in their own country was destroyed. This was perhaps the first time that Malay reaction was not typically Malay. It is probable that it was the suddenness of the proposal which shocked the Malays out of their stupor.

After their success in opposing the citizenship proposals of the Malayan Union plan, it was perhaps logical to expect the Malays to consolidate their position. Their strength during the struggle against the Malayan Union was considerable and a firm stand on the question of citizenship could have been taken. The practice in other parts of the world was not unknown to them and could have been used in their favour. The fear of being reduced to an underprivileged minority in their own country was still too real to allow them to cease their opposition to extension of citizenship to others. Yet, contrary to all expectations, when new moves were made to give citizenship rights to immigrants who were not only of questionable loyalty but were actually hostile to them, the Malays did not react as they had done to the shock of the Malayan Union citizenship proposals. They saw the thin end of the wedge, they recognized it, and yet they did almost nothing about it. A study of the citizenship changes which have taken place since the Malayan Union proposals will show that the wedge was driven in with almost clockwork regularity. At each stage, and at every change in the Constitution, the number of Malay citizens of the country became less and less in comparison with those of immigrant origin. Today, the citizenship situation is almost the same as would have obtained had Malayan Union been accepted by the Malays. But although they were aware of it, they did not react as they did before. They were once again their old selves. The wedge is still being driven in but we can expect the Malays to sit back and leave things to fate. Some even go so far as to say that this is no longer their country but belongs to whoever cares to claim it. Some say that even if they were the original people and the definitive citizens, they have no right to impose and control citizenship qualifications irrespective of the practice elsewhere.

The leadership of the Malays has always tended to be liberal. The followers are not usually so. The rumblings of discontent are already heard. To the ordinary Malays, citizenship for aliens still carries the same threat of

151

domination by others. They know their rights, and it is neither wise nor fair to disregard these rights. On the question of citizenship, their problem is to make known their attitude without causing embarrassment and without precipitating a crisis. This is a difficult task, and it is possible they might fail. If this happens, the result might be disastrous for all. It is far better that the problem is tackled now and this dilemma of the Malays appreciated. Citizenship in Malaya must conform with the pattern of citizenship elsewhere. Citizenship must carry obligations as well as privileges. Citizenship must be accepted as a sign of recognition and not as an inducement. It is only thus that the sincerity of the neo-citizens can be proved. And it is thus that the tide of Malay disappointment and dissatisfaction can be stemmed and a Malaysia built on a truly loyal citizenry.

Had the Malays in the past pointed out that they are the definitive people and that, as in other countries, this conferred on them a certain say in language, immigration, national education and citizenship, then the problems that beset national unity would not have become so aggravated and aggravating. The distinctive characteristics of the citizens would have been achieved. Once this homogeneous community was formed, many problems would have disappeared. But, as it is, communalism is likely to be a permanent feature of Malaysia. This division of citizens, which is a true division caused by not only language and culture but also by occupation, economic well-being, habitat, educational background, values and even way of thinking, will always be accompanied by a whole series of problems, and this will always be a source of intercommunal tension.

In other countries language, immigration, citizenship and national education are the major factors which definitive people insist on controlling. In addition the national religion and culture are also those of the definitive people. Thinking on religious beliefs however seems to have changed, and there is seldom insistence that new citizens must follow the religion of the definitive race. The culture of the definitive race is perpetuated through control of language, immigration, citizenship and education. In any case, culture changes with the times, and these changes, once the other factors have had their full effect, will involve the whole community and will therefore retain the homogeneous nature of the citizens with the essential characteristics of the definitive race.

In pushing into the background the claims of the Malays as the definitive people of the Malay Peninsula, the initial chance to mould a homogeneous citizenry was missed. The present policies are not likely to succeed in bringing the races together. Divisions will therefore continue and will be a permanent source of conflict. My purpose in pointing out what has been neglected is that repairs may be done here and there whenever the opportunity arises. This situation raises many problems affecting mainly the Malays who, because of character and circumstance, have become the have-nots in their own land. Problems have to be spotlighted now so that remedies can be sought while a solution is still possible. To ignore these problems is to permit their growth and to render them insoluble. Only disaster could follow such a short-sighted course.

9: Code of Ethics and Value Systems of the Malays

A race is distinct not only because of its physiognomy, language and usual habitat, but also because of its culture. Culture is deeply interwoven with the code of ethics and value systems of a given race. It is these ethics and value systems which give rise to the literature, the visual and creative arts and other manifestations of what normally constitutes culture. More importantly the ethical codes and value systems determine the progress and development of a race under a given set of circumstances.

The ethical codes and value systems of the Malays have never been studied and analyzed. Certainly few Malays care to comment on these sensitive topics. Yet if we are ever going to tackle the problems of the Malays and of Malaysia with any hope of success, it is imperative that we know why, under a given set of conditions, the Malays react and progress so differently from the Chinese and others.

While my thoughts on this subject may be neither scientific, nor amount to a study in depth, I have tried to throw light on a matter that is little understood though frequently mentioned. If nothing else, they might at least help others to understand the Malays better.

Values and value systems affect the development and progress of all human communities. Generally the value concepts of a given society are taken for granted except by sociologists and behavioural scientists. It is only when human societies or communities come into contact with each other, and the differing values conflict and lead in different directions, that these values become of interest to the average person.

Value concepts and ethical codes are closely related. As ethical codes are greatly influenced by religion or the interpretation of religion, it follows that values too are

154

closely connected with religious beliefs. Thus, the progress of Western countries is believed to be due to the Judaeo-Christian code of ethics. Certainly it is not difficult to relate the rapid expansion of Islam after the death of the Prophet to the changed values that Islam brought to the Believers. From Spain to China, the armies of Islam fought to bring the faith to what then constituted the world. The extension and development of the same Islamic code led to advances in science and the humanities after an initial period of conquest.

An understanding of the value systems and ethical codes of the Malays is therefore a prerequisite for the planning of their future. A study of these values may prove discouraging. But without some understanding of them, not only will it be impossible to correct wrong ideas due to incorrect interpretation, but plans for Malay progress would founder because they would conflict with established values.

Islam is the greatest single influence on the Malay value concepts and ethical codes. But it is important to remember that it is not so much the religion, but the interpretation of the doctrines of Islam which has the most significant effect. Interpretation of religions varies not only with the individual but with the age and the time, and even the country. It is relevant to note that Islam itself has five important sects, and that a new sect frequently appears due to some individual interpretation. If at times the influence of Islam appears to be adversely affecting Malay value concepts, it must be borne in mind that it is not so much Islamic teaching as its local contemporary interpretation which causes these adverse effects.

Again the value concepts of Islam in Malaysia are affected by the much older faiths of the Malays. Some, especially animism, have a much greater hold on the rural than the urban Malays. The influence of these faiths is therefore still considerable in the rural areas, and at times it runs counter to Islam. Apart from religious faith, Malay civilization has thrown up a comprehensive and rather formidable code of behaviour and forms of ceremony which go by the name of *adat* or custom. *Adat* itself appears to be influenced by the past and present religions of the Malays, but there is a considerable portion of it which appears to be unique and quite unrelated to any faith. The influence of *adat* has waned, but is still considerable in the more conservative rural areas, which, as we must keep in mind, is where most Malays live.

Contact with the non-Malay world has also influenced the value systems of the Malays. This contact may be divided into two; that is, with the non-Malay Muslim world of which the most significant is contact with the Arab world both at home and abroad; and contact with the non-Muslim people, the Europeans, the Chinese and others. By and large, the influence which these inter-racial contacts have on Malay values is less when faiths differ than when religious faiths are similar. The contact with a few Arabs has had a much greater impact on Malay values than that with all the other non-Muslim races put together.

Ethical codes and value concepts or systems are large subjects which cannot be fully covered in any single study. As the object of this exercise is to try and relate the cause and effect of the problems affecting the Malays in a larger study, only those codes and concepts which are relevant to the problem need to be dealt with. However, before going on it is worth finding out what the Malays think of the basis of ethics, the concept of good.

The first thing which strikes the observer is the distinct difference between the professed code and the actual practice of ethics. Equally striking is the apparent failure by the Malays themselves to notice this difference. Thus, observation of actual practice would give one set of values, while direct interrogation would reveal quite a different set of ideas. To varying degrees this is universal, but it would be wrong not to note this at the beginning in order to avoid criticisms of seemingly contradictory observations later on.

On the basic concept of good the Malays seem to fall in with the Kantian idea of uprightness. What is good is not what is pleasant but what is proper. What is proper is laid out in the strict religious code of Islam and of *adat*. To be well thought of is good for the community and is also good for the individual, but generally the individual is regarded as secondary to the community.

Formality and ritual rate very high in the Malay concept of values. What is formal is proper. To depart from formality is considered unbecoming, rude and deserving of misfortune or punishment by God and man. This is essentially a conservative attitude. It does not condone innovations. It certainly does not encourage change and inventiveness. There is always a proper way to do things and it is not expected that there should be a logical explanation of why the prescribed way is correct and acceptable. As religion is the main basis of the Malay system of values, it is natural that virtue and wisdom are synonymous with religious piety. To be learned in religion is good, admirable and worthy of respect. Learning increases with age and therefore in Islam the greatest respect is accorded the old and the learned.

Hedonism as such has no place in the Malay code of ethics. Pleasure, whether physical or mental is considered base. Nothing is done for the sake of pleasure alone. To serve one's fellowman may give satisfaction and pleasure, but that is not why a Malay should be of service to others. It is only duty and propriety which move him. The moving force is to appear right in the eyes of God and man. In other words, a deed is done because it is proper and not because it is pleasant or because it gives one the pleasure of achievement. Physical pleasure is regarded as lowly and must be suppressed or at least hidden. Eating good food in excess is frowned upon, and the drinking of intoxicating drinks is forbidden by religion and partly by public disapproval.

There is no Malay equivalent to the epicurean philosophy of "eat, drink and be merry". Life is transient and is a time when one prepares for the hereafter. Worldly life is therefore dedicated not to pleasure or merriment but to serious religious thought and obedience to the injunctions of religion. To be too preoccupied with worldly things, such as the accumulation of wealth, is bad. If the Malays are not epicureans, they are also not quite stoics. Life is a series of suffering, but it is not expected that all suffering must be endured stoically. A certain bending with the wind under adverse conditions is expected. Even with religion it is enjoined that rather than endure the pain of torture one should at least make a show of giving up one's faith. The Christian martyrs who would die rather than deny their faith are regarded by Malays as being unnecessarily foolish. The outward manifestations of faith are sometimes unimportant as religion is a matter of the soul. To be stoical and to endure pain for the sake of outward appearance is foolish and lacking in merit.

However in contradiction to the religious injunction to outwardly bend with the wind is the adherence to form as prescribed by *adat*. In the Malay code of behaviour, form is so important that it is preferred to the actual substance. Thus, the formality of official status is regarded as more important than the authority which should go with it. In other words, it does not matter if it is not so, so long as it appears to be so. This attitude explains the success and the ease with which the British took over the Malay states, ruling them as protected states in form, but in substance treating them as colonies.

Finally, there is the fatalism which characterizes the Malay attitude to life. This fatalism is very much in evidence everywhere and greatly affects the whole Malay value concept. It makes acceptance of everything, whether good or bad, possible with unprotesting tolerance and resignation. It does not encourage any great effort to change. It does not encourage resistance and certainly it does not engender a rebellious spirit. If an attempt is made at all to do anything, failure is accepted with resignation. This whole philosophy is contained in the Malay axiom —"*Rezeki sa-chupak tak akan jadi sa-gantang*", or "One's lot of a quart will never become a gallon." In other words fate decides all and to strive to better one's lot is useless unless fate wills such betterment.

The effect of this resignation to fate is to relegate the struggle for worldly goods to a low priority. Pride in working to one's utmost ability and capacity is not common. Nor is there any great admiration for the man who refuses to give up working because of a handicap or because of old age. The correct and acceptable attitude is one of sad recognition of the limitations of one's capacity and a willingness to submit to these limits. There should be visible sympathy from others for the less fortunate. This is an admired and common trait among Malays.

Before going on to discuss the common events in the experience of man in his environment and the attitude of the Malays to these events, it is perhaps worthwhile recapitulating these general remarks on Malay ethical values to see how they stand vis-a-vis the ethical values enunciated by the philosophers of antiquity. The first thing that can be said of Malay ethics is that it has not been influenced by a conscious knowledge of these ancient ethical philosophies. Any similarity to, or any obvious rejection of the values of the ancient Greeks and the Mediterranean civilization prior to the Christian era must therefore be purely coincidental.

In the first place, self-examination which occupied so much of the attention and the time of the Greek philosophers is not regarded as a great virtue. Deliberate critical self-analysis is therefore uncommon. Socrates' interpretation of the Delphic Oracle's "Know thyself" which makes a virtue of knowledge of self has no equivalent among the Malays. This does not apply to the individual only, but to the community as well. This failure produces an inability to find and correct the faults within. The more conservative the society, the more pronounced is this failure. This is the most marked in rural societies, and results in complete failure to relate cause to effect.

The kind of knowledge which is revered is religious knowledge. The pursuit of religious knowledge is quite remarkable, especially in the so-called backward rural areas. The Quran for example is widely read, interpreted and discussed. Among the Malays, a command of Arabic is common, and occasionally even Urdu, the language medium of Islamic teaching in Pakistan and India, is understood.

However, it is the spiritual values of Islam which appeal most. The emphasis is on a saintly life, a life free of sin, a life which is most likely to result in a happy after-life. Religious knowledge is therefore acquired for the sake of religious knowledge and to lead one to a life of piety. But the virtue of knowledge derived from religion is not always carried through to influence other values. Of Plato's three cardinal virtues, temperance is most marked among the Malays. Temperance is not an active philosophy but is more a product of the climatic and geographical environment of the Malays. The intemperate man is not admired. The impression given is one of continuous restraint which taxes the will. It seems to lead to an inner conflict, and at times the restraining bonds seem to burst and suddenly the polite formality disappears to be replaced by a violent outburst that is frightening in its intensity.

Nevertheless, the average Malay usually desires and leads a temperate life. In his enjoyment of the pleasures of life, in his attitude to others and in his reaction to his circumstances and surroundings, there is always this quality of moderation. The good Malay is always unobtrusive and self-effacing, unwilling to impose his will if it conflicts with others, and ever willing to compromise.

Courage, the second of Plato's cardinal virtues, acquires a meaning quite different from the concept of courage in the whole Western history of ethics. The firmness of will in aggression, in withdrawal or in endurance directed by a true insight into a situation, as described by Plato, is not a part of the Malay make-up. Firmness in fact is not a Malay characteristic at all. The type of courage which requires firmness and adherence to a principle is therefore uncommon among Malays. Courage in most instances is equated with a willingness to face up to a hopeless situation. It is facing up to overwhelming odds which could certainly lead to defeat and destruction. To take on an adversary when it seems to be beyond one's capacity is courageous. To calculate and assess one's chances first is to exhibit cowardice. Time and again this inability or unwillingness to measure the odds against them has led to defeat and disaster for the Malays. The courageous or brave Malay is usually foolhardy, and because he is likely to do things without thinking of the consequences, the average Malay treats him with fear and respect. The ordinary man knows that it is not worthwhile to incur his displeasure and that it is safer to let him have his own way. The ordinary man therefore represents the other extreme when principle is easily set aside for the sake of safety.

These remarks may sound derogatory. There have been many instances of true courage in the history of the Malays. The heroic exploits of some members of the Malay Regiment are common knowledge. But the generalization is basically correct. It explains why Malays are adept in overcoming the enemy by stealth and cunning, and the infrequency of frontal assault in any situation.

Wisdom as defined by Plato is not the wisdom accepted by the Malays. The need to control desires and to direct will-power is recognized, but wisdom is regarded mainly as the ability to circumvent a given situation. It is not restraint or direction which are highly regarded, but ability to avoid a clear cut decision and to be able to make corrections later on which are acclaimed. The Malay is never committed to anything. There is always a loophole somewhere for his escape. In trying to perfect an escape route for a given situation, decision making often becomes a tedious and time-consuming process. Indeed, where possible, a decision is avoided completely, thus preparing the ground for a reversal and later justification.

It is clear that Plato's three cardinal virtues do not apply to the Malays. These virtues are present, but because their values are different, the society they mould is totally different, and has not evolved along the same lines as Western civilization. And, because Malay value concepts and code of ethics, are different from those of the West, it is unlikely that mere changes in environment will bring about the necessary change in Malay values to such an extent that they will be able to compete with the drive of other communities or races. In other words, without a radical change in their code of ethics and value concepts, the efforts to effect a mass cure of the ills afflicting the Malays will merely increase the general frustration of all concerned, as the results obtained would be minimal.

Let us now examine the Malays' attitudes to the common experience of human society; to life and death, to the individual and the community, to wealth and poverty and to other major events which affect thinking and reactions in society. Life is a gift of God and the most valuable gift man possesses. The Malays value life but do not seem to fully appreciate what constitutes life and what its purpose is. Because life is a gift of God it must not be taken away. To kill is bad but it is even worse to take one's own life. Hence suicide is rare, and those who commit it are a cause of shame to the surviving relatives. Since taking life is bad, the Malay will hardly ever kill deliberately. The frequency with which murders occur in a Malay community is due to fits of temper. Murders are seldom planned and very rarely is it difficult to trace the assailant.

Despite this apparent reverence for life, the Malays do not seem to know what to do with it. In the more conservative rural communities life is almost exclusively a period of preparation for the hereafter. It is doubtful that this is what is enjoined by Islam. It is more likely that this attitude is a form of escapism from the realities of life, an insulation against the envy the Malays must feel for the prosperity of other races and other countries. The result of this dedication to the hereafter is that the Malays can convince themselves that they are not missing anything in life if they do not have worldly goods. Life is temporary while the hereafter will be permanent. If life is temporary and a better life awaits a man, then too much determination to live is neither worthwhile nor becoming. This is of course a fatalistic attitude. The will to live and to struggle for a better life can never be very strong if this is the dominant attitude.

Life is related to time. To live is to exist for a period of time. Life and time are therefore inseparable. If life is valued, time must also be valued. Unfortunately this relationship between life and time does not seem to be appreciated by the Malays. Life is valuable but time is not. Time is therefore wasted or completely disregarded. Age, for example is extremely flexible. The average Malay is vague about his own age and any guess by him is likely to be far in excess of actuality. This is because age is venerated and a man or even a woman must claim to be older all the time. A man could carelessly claim to be a hundred years old when a simple check will reveal he is no more than seventy.

Disregard for time is seen in the careless way in which it is spent. Doing nothing, or sipping coffee, or talking is almost a Malay national habit. An invitation to a *khenduri* in a kampong is invariably for an indefinite time. One may arrive at any time, eat at any time and go off at any time. No one ever arrives on time for a meeting but once started there is no limit to the time it can last. A meeting would therefore start late and end even later, no matter how much the time of the meeting is adjusted to suit everyone.

When there is no awareness of time, there can be no planning and work is never reliable. A time-table is an essential part of the life of modern man. Indeed, the more technologically advanced the man, the more he is bound to time. The count-down symbolizes the absolute dependence of modern technology on time. Without mathematically perfect timing man would never have conquered space. A community which is not conscious of time must be regarded as a very backward society. What is more, it will remain a backward society. It can never achieve anything on its own and it can never be expected to advance and catch up with superior time-conscious civilizations. There is no doubt that the Malay failure to value time is one of the most important handicaps to their progress.

This attitude to life and time represents a contradiction in the Malay value system. On the one hand life is valued highly yet on the other, time, which must go with life in order to make life significant, is not highly valued. Time is wasted and by extension life is wasted too. If life is a divine gift then time too must be a divine gift. To waste time is surely not a proper way for people who have deep religious beliefs and appreciate this gift of God. Yet this is the way that time is treated by the Malays. Time is wasted and so life too is wasted. The deep veneration of life is therefore somewhat nullified by this failure to give the same value to time.

To the Malays, whether deeply religious or not, death is the time when a man pays for the wrongs he has done in his life, and receives the rewards for his good deeds and religious piety. Because no man can honestly say to himself that he has done nothing but good in his life, and because he must be punished for any wrong that he has done throughout his life, death, even for the deeply religious, must hold a lot of unknown fears. The Malay fears death but paradoxically he cannot bring himself to struggle against it. His is the attitude of the fatalist. He resigns himself to his own death and to the death of others. He seeks solace in prayer. He delivers himself completely to the mercy of God, for he is not prepared to do anything more for himself. Nevertheless, despite this fatalistic acceptance of death, the realization that death must come to him shocks the Malay. This realization, which usually comes when he passes thirty-five or forty, often results in severe neurosis and affects his whole attitude to life. He becomes extremely cautious, avoids anything that is in the least bit dangerous, and finds difficulty in facing the problems of life. Often he withdraws into himself and refuses to make any great effort for worldly well-being.

Death, when it comes, is accepted calmly by the Malay. It is also accepted without much ado by his closest relatives and his friends. Sometimes there even appears to be an anxiety to die, so that as soon as a man is fairly sick, he and his relatives quietly make preparations for death. Seeking medical aid is not something done as a matter of course. A prolonged debate is held between relatives, friends and even the sick person. No one wants to accept the responsibility of making a decision, especially a decision to do something positive. No one wants to be accused later that he was responsible for doing something which might have had some bearing on the death, or worse still, which might have caused death. The debate is often inconclusive while the patient slowly slides towards death.

And as the invalid patiently awaits a decision which might help him to get well, friends and relatives stream in to offer their sympathy. Unfortunately this gesture has become so formalized that it is no different from attending a minor feast. It is customary to serve coffee to visitors and this is done even though it imposes an extra strain on the patient's household. The visitors, after formally enquiring of the patient, sit around and carry on light conversation. At the slightest sign of approaching death, prayers are read. Death, when it comes finally, is accepted calmly by the relatives. There is no wailing. The closest relatives may sob quietly but for the most part death appears to be a relief. There is no very great distinction between the death of an old man and the death of a child or a young man. All deaths are the same, a pre-ordained thing which one can do very little about and which one accepts as fated.

Muslim teaching is against elaborate funerals and memorials. What is being buried is just the body, and the body of man is just so much dirt and therefore of no consequence. The soul is not buried with the body and the perpetuation of the site of burial is not important. Graves are dug at the sites of old graves and old tombstones are discarded. The deceased is not eulogised at his burial. A common prayer is read for all. After that only the womenfolk care to visit the graves to read verses from the Quran on Friday mornings and during the festivals of Id.

Death is, therefore, feared by the Malays but when the time comes they accept it calmly. The dead man is soon forgotten and nothing is done to perpetuate his memory. Death, except for death met in a religious war, is not glorious. But religious wars no longer happen, and therefore death may not be courted. When men fear death, the deliberately careless adventure-seeking type of bravery is uncommon. But when this fear is paradoxically coupled with an acceptance of the inevitability of death, then blind courage in the face of overwhelming odds is common. It is this that makes the Malays, normally so self-effacing and submissive, suddenly lash out without the slightest fear of the certain destruction they invite. The *amok* is partly the result of the Malay attitude towards death.

The attitude to property and money is the key to the economic and social progress of a human community. An understanding of the Malay attitude to property and money is therefore necessary in order to attempt to better the condition of the Malays which is comparatively poor and backward. Property is acquired or inherited. For most Malays property and land are almost synonymous. Land constitutes most of the property Malays own, since the Malays are largely peasants. The process of acquiring land is still basically traditional.

In the old Malay sultanates, a Malay could acquire a piece of land if he could show evidence that he had settled on the land, cleared it and cultivated it. Permission to clear and settle was not asked first. A Malay merely picked land that was obviously unoccupied, and without further formality set about settling on it. After a few years he then applied for, and fully expected the right to a grant title in perpetuity to the land. And, in the old Malay states, this right was respected and upheld and in due course a grant title in perpetuity was issued.

Work was definitely involved in acquiring landed property, but the simplicity of the process did not make for much initiative and ingenuity. Anyone could acquire property if he so wished. What was even more telling in the attitude of the Malays was that there was a feeling of a right to property. This feeling promoted complacency and minimized any effort at self-enrichment. The most important thing in the process of acquiring property was not the work and the initiative, but the decision to acquire the property.

Land grants were almost invariably given to the Malays in perpetuity by the sultanates. Land once alienated becomes inheritable property, and eventually landed property is fragmented according to Muslim law. But attachment to the land as truly real property is deeply ingrained, and proprietorship of land becomes a status symbol, no matter

166

how small or uneconomic the piece of land might be. Land may also be acquired by financial transaction. Direct pur-chase of land does occur, but this has always been unusual. Usually land which is not inherited is acquired in the process of *jual janji,* a usurious practice that should be thoroughly condemned as being not only unethical but also un-Muslim. In this practice, a man pledges his land to another in order to borrow money. The amount involved is usually a fraction of the value of the land. Failure to pay within the stipulated time usually means that the land is acquired by the lender.

Land dominates the Malay mind and is the property most often involved in disputes. Such disputes become emotional issues. Rights to a piece of land may bring about acrimon-ious legal wrangles during which the money spent in getting a court ruling may exceed by several times the actual value of the land. But to all the parties in the dispute the money is well-spent. The satisfaction derived from a closely fought legal battle justifies the expenditure of the money.

Apart from land, the Malays have very little else that they regard as property. Jewellery and actual cash may sometimes constitute property, but the ease with which money and jewellery can be disposed of or just hidden and the lack of documentary evidence of title prevents these items from being accumulated as permanent inheritable possessions. Money is a convenience to the Malays. Money facilitates the exchange of goods and services. Money is not generally regarded as capital for investment. Whatever money is acquired, is acquired by selling property or services. The whole proceeds of the sale are then avail-able for changing for services or for outright spending.

This inability to understand the potential capacity of money is what makes the Malays poor businessmen. Beyond selling what they produce in work or in kind, the Malays appear unable to devise ways of acquiring money. It is true that money must be spent even in growing padi, but this involvement of money is minimal. Seeds are kept over from the previous crop. If the cultivator is a tenant he has paid off the rent with his crop. Preparation of the land is mainly by self labour. Fertilizer is acquired through promises to sell the harvest to the local Chinese shop. Labour for transplanting is on a *gotong-royong* basis with only food being provided to the neighbours who help. Even harvesting is mainly paid off in food. What little money is paid out comes from advances made by the local Chinese millers.

The minimal use of money makes an understanding of costing extremely poor. Business is mainly an appreciation of cost and pricing in accordance to cost. *Gotong-royong,* good neighbours and haphazard cash advances, together with a failure to put a money value on self-labour make a computation of costs impossible. In addition to all these, the income from the next crop has usually been spent through unbudgeted credits in kind from the local provision shop. Actual handling and counting of money is minimal. Padi planting is therefore never a business proposition. It is a way of life.

The urban Malay is only slightly better. But again with him money is a convenience for spending. It is earned in the form of salary, and in the main it is almost completely spent. Savings are minimal and often the hire-purchase system means that money is spent well ahead of its being earned. It is only the few Malays involved in business who can understand the sophistication of a monetary system and how it could be made to work to earn a larger income. One aspect of monetary transaction which has attracted considerable attention since the move by the Malays to break into commerce and industry is the acceptance of interest on loan. Islam forbids usury. The local interpretation of usury includes even the smallest interest on loans. Needless to say this interpretation blocks Malay involvement not only in money-lending but also banking. Usury is undoubtedly a cause of much human misery. It is easy to understand why Islam forbids it. However while lending at exorbitant interest is forbidden to Muslims, borrowing is permissible. In a country with a mixed Muslim and non-Muslim population, this double-standard leads to Muslims borrowing from usurious non-Muslim money-lenders. The injunction of Islam against usury is thus unable to prevent the misery that is the lot of the borrower. At the same time the disapproval of lending with even the smallest interest prevents the Malays from enjoying the profits from this type of monetary transaction. The value of money to the Malays lies mainly in its ability to facilitate the acquisition of goods and services. The monetary system is still primitive, being merely a slight extension of the barter system. Budgeting, savings, banking, investments, credits, growth, transfers and all the other refinements in the use of money are generally not appreciated.

Malay values with regard to property and money may therefore be said to be undeveloped. A prosperous society depends very much on the ability of its members to manipulate money and to equate property not with land holdings alone, but with less and less tangible assets which may include prestige and goodwill in business. Failure to appreciate the real value of money and property is equivalent to not subscribing to the materialism of the modern world. In itself this is not a bad thing if the particular society is completely isolated from the materialistic world. High spiritual values make for a happier and more contented life. But where the materialists are juxtaposed with those inclined to high spiritual ideals, the impact of the former invariably damages the social order of the latter.

The Malays are not completely isolated. Even in the remotest Malay village, while social isolation is complete, economic isolation is impossible. On the other hand even the urban Malays are not and will not be socially fully integrated with non-Malays. At the same time urban Malays, while their value systems have undergone some change, still retain a great proportion of the same value system as rural Malays. Generally therefore the undeveloped or underdeveloped value systems of the Malays with regard to money and property work to the disadvantage of the Malays in the multiracial country in which they live.

Social codes give character to a community. They are both the product and the cause of the value system of the community. This makes analysis very difficult, for in any particular instance it is not easy to determine whether it is the value system which produces the social code, or whether it is the social code which affects the value system. Nevertheless an insight into the social codes of the Malays should throw some additional light on the value which mould and shape the progress of the Malay race.

First and foremost, the feudal nature of Malay society. Rank is important, and with rank go a number of privileges. The highest rank is that of the ruling princes, the hereditary rajas of the Malay states. Even among Malays who have been to foreign countries, are educated in the western ways of life and are acquainted with western values, an acceptance of the hereditary rulers is general. Obeisance to the rajas is practised as a matter of course. It is a mark of breeding to know how to behave towards the rajas. This code of behaviour includes the use of a whole range of special words regarding the person of the raja and his family. Indeed as the title of *Tunku,* or prince, is lavishly used by the descendants of every raja, past and present, contact between the *ra'ayat* and royalty is common and few Malays remain unfamiliar with the tabooed language, the special privileges and accepted codes of behaviour towards the rajas. Politeness and formality engendered by close contact between. different ranks thus become very much a part of Malay life. A desire to be very polite has however resulted in an extension of this code of behaviour to persons of high rank, real or imaginary, other than the raja's family or relatives. Thus the *Syeds,* the descendants of the prophets, are accorded a high degree of respect. In some states *Syeds* are as privileged as royalty and remain a race apart. Below these hereditary ranks are numerous other classes of people with varying degrees of privileges. Foreigners, officials, members of the various legislatures and village chiefs are all titled and given the respect which is considered their due.

In itself the feudalist inclination of the Malays is not damaging. It makes for an orderly law-abiding society. People who could follow and observe an unwritten code of behaviour are easily made to observe the written laws of a country. People who accept that a society must have people of varying degrees of authority and rights easily make a stable society and nation. A revolution in such a society is unusual unless led from above. A feudal society is therefore not necessarily a dormant or retrogressive society. It can be a dynamic society if there is dynamism at the top. But when the top fails, or is preoccupied with its own well-being, the masses become devoid of incentive for progress.

The formality and painstaking politeness of the Malays make frankness rare. It is impossible to be extremely polite and courteous without being self-denying and humble as well. Good manners demand that criticism be minimal or at worst indirect. The net result of this self-restraint is that the Malays are invariably misinterpreted. Thus, when the Malays call foreigners *tuan*, or "master", out of politeness, they are apt to be taken literally. The Malays, on finding that those whom they politely call "master" have in fact assumed the attitude of masters towards them, are restrained by politeness from pointing out the obvious mistake. The Malay social code contributes greatly to making the Malays what they are today. Self-restraint and a desire not to displease does not make for an aggressive society. The world is getting more and more rude. Frankness is the order of the day. In politics as much as in the sciences there is a growing dedication to facts. Old ideas, half-truths and adulation of form are giving way before the pragmatism of the modern approach. For the most part the Malay social code is therefore somewhat anachronistic and can only lessen the competitive abilities of the Malays and hinder their progress.

Frankness, therefore, is not a part of the Malay social code. This analysis and criticism of Malay values, largely disparaging as it must seem, is uncharacteristic and atypical of a Malay. In modern psychology seeking out and identifying causes serves not only to facilitate treatment but is also part of the treatment. There is an almost immediate relief when a cause is identified. From then on it is a question of either removing the cause or nullifying or reversing its effect. The process of identifying the cause is often painful and depressing. Events are recalled which seem far better forgotten. Yet without this laborious and painful process, treatment cannot begin. And so it is with the ailments of a community. To cure, it is imperative that the painful process of identifying the causes of the ailment be examined. A therapy based on the successful experience and methods of others will have minimal or no effect. There is no other way but to face boldly the pain of self-examination, the admission that one is wrong, and the acceptance that the cure lies in the rejection of some ideas and concepts no matter how dear to the heart they may be.

This critical analysis and evaluation of the value system of the Malays is painful and fraught with the danger of causing either an inferiority complex or excuses for past failures. But, in the desperate situation in which the Malays find themselves, there is little choice. Traditional politeness has apparently failed. There may be harm in the rude frankness that characterizes the value system of Western civilization, but as the world seems to be dominated by Western or Western oriented people, and as those who have adjusted to Western values have survived and done well, it would seem worthwhile trying some of the ways of the West in order to get at the root of the failure of the Malays to compete with others.

This examination of the value system and ethical codes of the Malays is therefore an attempt at a therapeutic diagnosis. It is an attempt to pinpoint the basic faults which must be corrected or adjusted in order that other measures to help the progress of the Malays may stand a better chance of succeeding. It is no good asking the Malays to go into business if they are not properly motivated and do not understand the functions and value of the monetary system. So long as he is a fatalist, the rural Malay will not struggle hard enough to preserve life and to succeed.

The value system and ethical code therefore determine the success or failure of corrective measures. If the value system is wrong, corrective measures will not be productive or will be only slightly productive. When the value system motivates, very little corrective measures are needed. This analysis of the value system of the Malays clearly shows that it hinders the progress and competitive abilities of the Malays in a multiracial society. True, not all the values are bad. The deep religious faith is good, for in itself it can be a motivating force. There is no reason why the Islamic faith, properly interpreted, cannot achieve spiritual well-being as well as material success for the Malays.

Even feudalism can be beneficial if it facilitates changes. The reason why animist Malays became Hindus is because their rajas became Hindus. Later when the rajas became Muslim the ra'ayat became Muslim. The political rajas of today can therefore institute change if they themselves are willing to change. Such a change would spread rapidly. If the indications are that there should be a change in the value system and ethical code, then the leaders can lead the way with the certainty that they will be followed by the masses. In a feudal society, if the leaders fail, then there is little hope for the masses.

By and large, the Malay value system and code of ethics are impediments to their progress. If they admit this, and if the need for change is realized, then there is hope; for as in psychiatry, success in isolating the root cause is in itself a part of treatment. From then on planning a cure would be relatively simple.

10: Communal Politics and Parties

Communalism has long existed, and despite claims to the contrary, there were no truly non-communal political parties in Malaysia. It was not until after the 1969 elections that most Malaysians learned just how serious the problem was.

In Malaysia today a lot of lip service is paid to the concept of non-communalism and above all to that of non-communal politics. The archetype of communal parties is the Pan Malayan Islamic Party, as well as the partners forming the Alliance.

Excluding the PMIP which makes no pretence at being non-communal, the other parties, including the partners of the Alliance, claim to be non-communal. But despite the vehemence of their protestations, all political parties are communal in their politics. Indeed, the more non-communal their set-up, the greater their communalist motivation. The only difference between the parties is their approach to the racial problem. One group believes in openly accepting racial differences and finding ways and means to minimize these differences in order to achieve an equitable society. Another group believes in ignoring the fact of racial differences, and in an atmosphere of instant equality between citizens, they pursue their politics which, in analysis, show to be extremely communal.

Both schools of thought are backed by the sincere, the naive and by plain knaves. As the obviously sincere do not appear to be considerable in number, it is natural that the two schools should be mutually suspicious. It is worthwhile discussing these two groups.

Let us take the "sweep it all under the carpet" school first. Protagonists of this school try to forget race and carry on as if there is no such thing. They point an accusing finger at the openly communal political parties and charge them with keeping race loyalties and communalism alive.

But is it so easy to forget race? Are the races in Malaysia unique in that they can easily forget their racial origins when we know that all over the world race or ethnic grouping is a *force majeur* both in internal as well as external politics? The evidence seems to indicate that Malaysia is not unique. Indeed Malaysians are more race conscious than most people, for Malaysians are Asians and Asians everywhere cling to race much more than Europeans or Africans. The white Americans or white Australians may originate from different parts of Europe but they are not often given to vaunting their racial origins. The American Negroes obviously came from different African tribes but none talk of being Watutsi, or Zulus or Kikuyus. But an Asian Indian in America is distinct from an Asian Chinese American or a Filipino American. They are not Asians. They are Indians, Chinese and Filipinos. They have not forgotten race for the simple reason that they are different.

In Malaysia we have three major races which have practically nothing in common. Their physiognomy, language, culture and religion differ. Besides, how is any one race going to forget race when each is in fact physically separated from the other? For the vast majority of the people in Malaysia there is no dialogue. Many of them are not even neighbours. They live apart in different worlds — the Chinese in the towns, the Malays in the *kampongs* and the Indians on the estates. Nothing makes anyone forget the fact of race. So those who say "forget race" are either naive or knaves.

If race differentiates citizens, then there must also be racial loyalty. Racial loyalty must involve privileges for one's race and denial of rights to others. Under these conditions each member of a race must be instinctively guided by considerations of profit and loss for himself. It follows that the more the privileges of a given race the greater the gain for the individual member. Each member must therefore seek to enhance the position of his race so that he himself may gain in the long run. If this fact of race, race loyalty and privilege are understood, then attitudes on race relations in Malaysia can be better appreciated.

175

By and large, the people who are most openly against the non-communal approach to politics are the Malays. If the pursuit of personal gain is the greatest driving force in all of us, then Malay objections to the non-communal approach must be mainly because they believe that they will lose. Are the Malays correct in assuming this?

There are spheres other than politics where the communal approach has been barred. In Government service, which is open to all races, the Malays have found difficulty in finding places. In the universities at home and abroad the Malays have not been able to find places.

Perhaps one could say that if you are no good you should not hold others up. The trouble is that the Malays are not absolutely no good. They are just comparatively not good enough for reasons connected with their value system and their background. This is nothing to be ashamed of. The Chinese in Japan are in the same position as the Malays. In Japan the Chinese are just not good enough whether in business or in skills. While Chinese everywhere in Southeast Asia have dominated or at least greatly influenced the local scene, the Chinese in Japan found themselves at a disadvantage when competing with the Japanese.

Because non-discrimination between races tends to work against the interest of the Malays, the Malays have to hang on to the system which affords them some bargaining power; thus they tend to depend on racialism to sustain themselves. If in the process they also block the advance of others, this too is nothing unusual. The days of the survival of the fittest are over. National as well as international mores now insist that there is an inherent right of the weak to be defended.

What would happen to this world if weak nations had no right to protect themselves against strong nations? The unequal strength which would follow would make strong nations stronger and the weak weaker. Tariffs and other laws prevent the small countries from being swallowed up by the big. In other words by open discrimination, the small countries are preventing the big countries from making their "natural" progress. The constant wrangling in general agreements on tariffs and trade, and the almost arrogant insistence by small nations that economically powerful nations should give them aid, are manifestations of modern thinking on human relations.

Internally, labour laws in most civilized nations reflect this same principle. If it is just a question of the ablest succeeding, then the rich and the powerful within a country would have every right to continue to advance their positions. But the gradual change in human values resulted in curbs being imposed on the more fortunate and new power given to the weak, and less fortunate, of society. Discriminatory income tax laws follow this same principle. The whole exercise is aimed at a more equitable society. No one is going to say that measures to create a more equitable society are wrong. Similarly it should not be wrong for the Malays to cling to a system which can elevate them to the status of other races, thus creating a more equitable society.

On the other hand, some non-Malays see the removal of racial politics as a means to enhance the position of their own race. So their cry against racial politics is in fact no echo of their racialist sentiments because removal of race politics and race discrimination would benefit them. The strategem is too transparent. The few Malays who want abolition of race politics are either simple or are unable to resist the offers of high positions in the so-called non-communal political parties. Other Malays refuse to be taken in.

Are the advocates of race politics racialists? Some of them no doubt are. But some maintain that only by taking the various races through protected stages to the point where all races are equal in all respects can there be true national unity. And when national unity is achieved, the need for race politics would disappear.

How valid is their argument? The races in Malaysia differ. One cannot ignore this fact. But what is more important is that each claims that the others are in a more advantageous position. The non-Malays point to Malay privileges. The Malays point to the economic hegemony of the Chinese. On the one hand, it requires but a stroke of the pen to deprive the Malays of the dubious privilege of living on reserves; on the other hand, nothing but enormous and unnatural self-restraint on the part of the Chinese over a very long period can break Chinese economic hegemony. Yet it is evident that without Chinese economic monopoly and Malay privileges, a more equitable society would result. An equitable society would promote racial integration. And of course if the races are integrated, not only would racial politics be anachronistic but racial political parties would fail to find enough support to survive.

The question is then reduced to one of whether the horse should come before or after the cart — whether by abolishing race, equality and integration would result, or whether by achievement of equality and integration, racial loyalties would disappear. It is difficult to believe that abolishing race would result in instantaneous equality and integration. Equality has to be established first for race loyalties to disappear and integration to take place.

If racial politics and racial political parties mean to achieve racial equality, then there is certainly a place for them in the affairs of Malaysia.

The politics of the parties constituting the Alliance, although basically racial, are apparently directed at achieving racial equality. Their existence do not jeopardise the efforts towards national unity. On the other hand the so-called non-communal parties are merely fronts for some of the most blatant racial politics. Their activities tend to be divisive and will not contribute towards the good of the nation. They are the harbingers of racial trouble, of unrest and of national retrogression.

178

11: Malaysia and Singapore

The Pyramid Club in Singapore is reputed to be the Think Tank of the PAP Government. It is no Rand Corporation, for its members are not at all like the detached scientists on whom the American Government relies so much. In fact, members of the Pyramid Club are very much involved in the day to day affairs of the Singapore Government. But there is no doubt that it serves the same purpose. And most certainly its members are the political and executive *elite* whose ideas and initiatives mould and make Singapore what it is today.

In January, 1969 I was asked to address members of this club on the subject of the future relationship between Malaysia and Singapore. The gathering (it was not a formal meeting or forum), was presided over by Mr S. Rajaratnam, Singapore's Minister of Foreign Affairs. Several other Ministers and high Government officials were among those present.

A lot of things have happened since then. The NOC Government which rules Malaysia today has become more nationalistic than the Alliance Government and appears less influenced by Singapore's peculiar relationship with Malaysia. In early 1970 it seemed more likely than ever that Singapore and Malaysia will draw further apart rather than closer together.

I have come to the conclusion that the question of re-unification of Malaysia and Singapore is no longer of consuming interest to the intellectuals of Singapore. This is significant because it marks a change in attitude and an acceptance of the fact of separation and its permanency. In Malaysia, separation has long been accepted as permanent. It would appear that at last, in a negative sort of way, Malaya has come to see eye to eye with Singapore.

I do not see reunification as the future relationship between Singapore and Malaysia. I was never keen on having

Singapore in Malaysia in the first place. I thought, after having spent six years in Singapore, that Singaporeans and Malaysians would not be compatible in a union. If reunification is out, then the only relationship between Malaysia and Singapore is the relationship between two sovereign nations. The relationship between sovereign nations is affected by a variety of factors — geography, history, ideology, ethnic origin, and language, as well as a host of other factors. In the final analysis, it is the will of the people as expressed by their chosen leaders that counts.

Let us systematically go through at least some of the factors that I have listed. Geography is of course important. We do not care much in Malaysia about what happens in Latin America. The reason is obvious. Our interest varies inversely with distance. Singapore, being a very close neighbour, interests us very much indeed. But proximity is not all. Size counts too. Geographically speaking Singapore's size is decisive.

When the British informed us that they wished to abdicate their role in this region by 1971, Singapore talked of shouldering her defence herself. Among the equipment Singapore spoke of acquiring were certain British-made jets. These jets fly at twice the speed of sound — roughly twenty-two miles a minute. In other words, it takes slightly less than one minute to fly across Singapore. This speed poses certain political and military problems. It means that these jets taking off in a northerly direction would be over Malaysian air space almost immediately after they became air-borne. Now air-space is sacred, especially when understanding is lacking. A hostile Malaysia would not take kindly to the regular infringement of its air-space by Singapore. Supposing Singapore is being attacked by a foreign power. The bombs could very well be launched while the planes are over Malaysian air-space — which means that unless Malaysia cooperates, the Hunter jets or even surface-to-air missiles would be pretty useless. The size of Singapore is therefore immensely important in determining the relationship between Singapore and

Malaysia. It is particularly important when the question of joint defence is involved.

The growth and importance of Singapore has been due in part to its strategic position in relation to the mainland. It was and still is, the natural port of the Malayan hinterland. If one is looking for a single dispersal point for the produce of Malaysia, no place is more suitable than Singapore. It is at the intersection of the sea routes to the East and the West, the South and the North. By the same token, it is also the most economic point of entry for goods destined for all parts of Malaysia. But it is not Singapore's position alone that makes it important to Malaya. The mountainous backbone of Malaya made east-west roads difficult. Hence the system of roads and railways in Malaya was built on either side of the mountain ranges, and these roads naturally converge on Singapore. Geographical factors make Malaya dependent on Singapore for purposes of commerce and trade. This in turn has led Singapore to set up extensive permanent facilities employing a considerable number of people to service Malaya's needs. Failure to utilize these facilities would hurt Singapore's economy. On balance, therefore, Singapore's need for Malaysia is greater than Malaysia's need for Singapore. Still, there is a considerable degree of interdependence and for the time being at least, friendship between the two nations should be beneficial to both.

Strained relations in the years following Singapore's independence forced Malaysia to develop Port Swettenham as her main West Malaysian port. Whereas in the past roads were built following the topographical configuration of the country, nowadays the only obstruction to the direction of roads is money. Malaysia is already busy building roads which radiate from Kuala Lumpur by the shortest routes to all the major towns of the north, the east and the south. Kuala Lumpur is linked with the North Klang Straits by Federal Route I. Once this system of roads is completed, Port Swettenham will become the nearest port to most of north and east Malaya. Only a part of the south will be nearer to Singapore. Thus the dominant geographical location of Singapore will not remain for long so far as Malaya is concerned. The use of Singapore as a Malaysian port will depend then not on geographical factors, but on policy.

Singapore will no doubt find ways and means to make herself less dependent on Malaysia for defence. But it seems that overcoming the limiting factor of geographical size is going to be slightly harder than solving physical problems in the building of roads.

Historically, the link between Malaya and Singapore is well-known. Singapore belonged to Johore until the Englishman Stamford Raffles installed a puppet sultan, and obtained a dubious concession. The puppet was later dropped when his usefulness was over. The main reason for the British takeover of Singapore was the weakness of the state of Johore. It had nothing to do with legality. The fact that Singapore is now an independent state has nothing to do with the history of Singapore in Malaya. It is no good therefore talking about historical links of systems of Government, of language of administration, of similarity of education etc. If these are important in influencing the relationship between nations, then the so-called British Commonwealth of Nations would be a solid united front. The fact is that history is made by people and the people who make history are not usually guided by the past, but by what is relevant during their lifetime. We can therefore ignore history when predicting the future relationship between Malaysia and Singapore.

The same cannot be said of ideologies. Ideologies and systems of Government now play a great part in either drawing nations together or repelling one from the other. The existence of blocs of nations is, for the most part, due to ideologies and systems of Government. Malaysia and Singapore are devoid of ideologies — or it can be said in a negative sort of way that the ideology of both countries is to be without ideology. This similarity is extremely important. If Singapore should become communist, and its potential for becoming communist is not yet exhausted, then Singapore would become thoroughly incompatible with

Malaysia. But Singapore has decided to maintain the outward appearance of a parliamentary democracy. Singapore is also pragmatic in its approach to problems. Singapore can also be accommodating. In all these things there are similarities with Malaysia. Malaysia is a parliamentary democracy. Malaysia is pragmatic and accommodating.

Malaysia and Singapore can therefore be close friends, partners in trade and possibly allies in peace and war. Unfortunately, ideologies and systems of Government, which can bring countries which are physically separated so close together, lose their effect somewhat when the countries are too close together or next-door neighbours. Other factors which mar the mutual sympathy of ideologies tend to intrude.

In the case of Malaysia and Singapore, the effect of non-ideologicalism and similarity of governmental system is marred by factors of race and personalities which proximity reveals. Singapore is essentially a Chinese nation with racial minorities, composed of people who have racial ties with the people of Malaysia. Malaysia on the other hand is a multiracial nation. Malaysia thus looks upon Singapore as a primarily Chinese nation, while it accuses Malaysia of being a Malay state.

I will not seek to justify the stand of Singapore or Malaysia. But the postures adopted by the two nations consequent upon these beliefs are not conducive to good relations. I told the Pyramid Club that Singapore, smarting from the indignity of separation, never missed an opportunity to run down Malaysia as a feudal state, spendthrift, inefficient and dominated by people unfit to govern. News-sheets, radio and T.V. played on this theme all the time. And in West Malaysia the remnants of PAP sympathizers kept up the debate which originally led to the separation of Singapore. In retaliation, Malaysia with characteristic inefficiency, tried to point out the lack of true democracy in Singapore, the one-party system which it practised, and the absolute dominance of the Chinese in Singapore.

Apart from this misunderstanding, due mainly to racial composition, the countries are close enough for the leaders to know each other well. The period of union made this personal contact even greater. This contact could have brought about better understanding between the leaders, but conflict of interests soon made each intolerable to the other. The conflict of interests became a conflict of personalities which affected the thinking of leaders on both sides of the causeway.

Even the most sanguine of observers must consider the present relationship between Malaysia and Singapore strained. It would seem, on looking back, that Singapore either did not understand what was meant by the separation which its leaders agreed to, or that Singapore hoped to rejoin Malaysia at a fairly early date. Whether it was misconception or hope, there is little doubt that Singapore did not examine the conditions of separation with care. Singapore's leaders are fond of saying that they never do anything without first calculating. In the case of separation, it would seem that either there was no calculation or it was done carelessly. There was, for example, the question of stationing Malaysian troops in Singapore. Then there was the agreement to call in Malaysian help in case of internal trouble in Singapore. The monetary system was to be the same, and there were a host of other important questions that Singapore never even bothered to bring up before separation was agreed to.

When Singapore came to realize the implication and the permanency of the separation, its leaders turned around and set for a collision course with Malaysia. Agreements made bilaterally were unilaterally rejected, and rejected in a manner that can only be described as unfriendly and provocative. It is true that most of the arrangements agreed upon by Singapore at the time of separation were to Malaysia's advantage. It is true that the conditions were hardly compatible with an independent, sovereign Singapore. It is true that these conditions had to be modified some time or other. But the manner in which Singapore went about reversing these agreed conditions was such as to make friendly relations difficult not only for the present but also for the foreseeable future.

As if reversing these agreed arrangements was not enough, Singapore thought up more provocative acts. It became rapidly harder for Malaysia to find justification for Singapore's actions. One of the most badly calculated decisions was to deport Malaysians working in Singapore. When we think of Singapore as the land of pen and paper calculators, the decision was even more incomprehensible. We all know what resulted from that decision.

Even so, Singapore has shown no desire to cease and desist. A typical example is the Malaysia-Singapore Airways affair. We admit that under present arrangements much of the profit of this bi-national airline is due to Singapore's air traffic. But it is important to remember that the airline's benefit accrues not only from the dividend it pays, but also the flow of foreign exchange and the employment it creates. Without the slightest shadow of a doubt, these advantages have accrued to Singapore out of all proportion to its share in the airline, or the profits Singapore brings in. Yet Singapore refuses to allow the employment of even a small number of Malaysians. Work permits were withheld from new employees and conditions made difficult for Malaysians already working in Singapore. What can happen to the airline can happen to almost any mutual arrangement between Singapore and Malaysia.

What of the future? What type of relationship could develop in future? Much depends upon the leaders.

Europe today is more homogeneous than it was ever thought possible, simply because most of its leaders think of its future rather than the past. In this context, Asia is about thirty years behind Europe. We are going through a phase of narrow nationalism which characterized Europe between the First and the Second World Wars. The concept of regional cooperation is still young. Like the Europe of the thirties, Asian nations are busy manoeuvring into positions of tactical superiority over neighbours, often aided by extra-continental friends. The only difference is that for the most part we do not have the capabilities for truly aggressive acts. We indulge in such ludicrous acts as passing laws annexing the territories of neighbours, knowing full well that we have no means of putting the laws into effect.

With this narrow nationalism characterizing Asia today and influencing the thinking of Malaysian and Singapore leaders, the only relationship which can result is one of destructive confrontation. The Singapore Foreign Minister for example thinks that beyond nationalism lies further nationalism. Far from thinking of an ideal united or at least co-existential world, the Foreign Minister is not even thinking of regionalism. From a Foreign Minister of a country which is a member of a regional organization, this does not spell much hope in terms of regional co-operation. This narrow nationalism seems to be a passing phase, and new leaders with greater vision will ultimately take over. But there seems little hope of this happening for a very long time.

A good proportion of Malaysia's trade goes through Singapore. In addition, innumerable firms have their head offices in Singapore, resulting in a concentration of money and spending in Singapore. At least one petroleum company has refineries in Singapore while selling its products in Malaysia. The classic example is MSA. All foreign earnings of this bi-national enterprises flow to Singapore. It may be said that Malaysia depends on Singapore for its commercial activity just as Indonesia also seems to depend on Singapore. But in the case of Malaysia, it is not lack of capacity but momentary convenience. The moment the services Singapore sells become too costly or incompatible with Malaysian independence, Malaysia can develop her own facilities.

Malaysia may not insist that a proportion of her nationals be employed in Singapore, but she certainly cannot tolerate harassment of her nationals. Besides, there are more Singaporeans working in Malaysia than Malaysians working in Singapore. The earnings of Singaporeans in Malaysia are far greater than the earnings of Malaysians in Singapore, since Malaysians there work as labourers and at other low-paid jobs. Singapore must know all this — being led as it is by the best brains — but nevertheless, Singapore decided to be extremely unreasonable. In the event "Operation Swop" proved the folly of this attitude. One would have thought that Singapore would cease harassing Malaysians and the Government of Malaysia, but as the MSA affair has shown, Singapore means to press every advantage it has. There are other areas where Singapore has shown itself equally uncooperative and even provocative.

In view of this attitude of Singapore, Malaysia has gone ahead with preparations which will cause Singapore to lose importance as a trading partner and probably even as a strategic defensive base. These are costly preparations, involving millions of dollars, contacting new trading partners abroad, and building permanent installations. Once they are operative, all these arrangements and installations must be maintained and fully utilized. It is most improbable that future friendship with Singapore will result in Malaysia abandoning her ports, her defence systems and her trade contacts abroad in order to re-establish the conditions which exist now.

If commercially and strategically Singapore is important to Malaysia, then the relationship between Singapore and Malaysia must depend almost entirely on the politics of the two nations. Singapore is an island in more ways than one. In the Malay archipelago, Singapore stands out like a sore thumb. Singapore's progress and prosperity must depend on, indeed must be at the expense of, her neighbours. The element of envy and jealousy on the part of Singapore's neighbours must be expected. Because of racial ties, the only true friend Singapore can expect is Malaysia. The only reason why the relationship between Malaysia and Singapore is not more strained than it is now, is because the Chinese in Malaysia wish to maintain good relations with Singapore.

But the Chinese in Malaysia understand the need to work with other communities in Malaysia. Efforts by Singapore to undermine the influence of these Chinese by stirring up Chinese chauvinism which can only thrive in Singapore, will produce resentment among Chinese Malaysians. If these Chinese Malaysians decide that friendship with Singapore is likely to work to their disadvantage in a Malaysia which is not commercially dependent on Singapore, then their effort to maintain ties with Singapore will cease. If on the other hand, Singapore ceases to create an unfavourable picture of Malaysia, then the prospect of friendly relations is good. Whether friendly relations without trade dependence will be to Singapore's liking is another question. But it is quite clear that what happens between Malaysia and Singapore depends very much on what Singapore chooses to do.